hEAVEN ON THE LINKS

Jim Croft

E ergreen
PRESS
An Imprint of Genesis
Communications, Inc.

Heaven on the Links
by Jim Croft

ISBN 1-58169-015-0
For Worldwide Distribution
Printed in the U.S.A.

Evergreen Press
An Imprint of Genesis Communications, Inc.
P.O. Box 91011 • Mobile, AL 36691
(334) 665-0022 • (888) 670-7463
Fax (334) 665-0570
Email: GenesisCom@aol.com

DEDICATION

This book is dedicated to Nabil Haddad, who introduced me to golf; Lucien Croft, my father and favorite playing partner; and my wife Prudence, who has never complained about my addiction to the game or the thousands I have spent playing it.

ACKNOWLEDGMENTS

I would like to thank Dr. Timothy Ford for his tireless work in helping me prepare the original manuscript for the publisher.

TABLE OF CONTENTS

Chapter One
MY FIRST TIME
A Golf Story

I played golf for the first time at age 41. I was vacationing with my family at the Fairfield Resort in Pogosa Springs, Colorado. Unbeknownst to us when we made the reservations, it was actually a golf resort that was built around one of the most beautiful championship courses in the state. After the first week, my wife, four daughters and I had enjoyed practically every recreational activity they had to offer, with the exception of golf. One morning, my wife said, "Take me golfing." Before that occasion, I had been an avid hunter who had declined scores of invitations to play golf. I was shocked that she would ask a "macho" man like myself to consider such a "wimpy" activity. Finally, she convinced me that it would be worthwhile, as it would give us an opportunity to see all the beautiful homes that lined the fairways. As I consented, I chuckled that the course was also surrounded by trees and that I was quite sure that she was subtly attempting to lure me into the woods. She responded with one of her "in your dreams" looks.

At the pro shop we paid what I thought was an outrageous amount of money for a cart, green fees and club rental. Then the attendant asked if we would be needing any balls or tees. I asked how they came and learned that balls came in sleeves of three or boxes of 12 and that tees came in little plastic bags of 25. I assured my wife that we would certainly not be needing more than three balls as there were only two of us playing. I reluctantly shelled out the cash for a sleeve of three bright orange Pinnacles and a 50-cent bag of tees. We launched out to play our first round without a clue as to the rules, etiquette or fundamentals of golf.

We were paired up with two experienced players. On the first tee, I discerned that closer was better, so we both hit from the ladies' tee box. I encouraged my wife to hit first. After multiple attempts, her ball was still resting on its tee staring defiantly up at her. I confidently announced that she could hit from wherever my ball landed. To my chagrin, when I finally made contact with my ball, it sliced pitifully and bounced into oblivion. We each took about 15 strokes before finally holing our putts on the first green. On the second tee, our partners mercifully offered instruction on the basics of the golf grip and swing. By the fifth hole we had exhausted our supply of balls and part of theirs, and they politely abandoned us.

We both were thoroughly mystified about how to succeed at the game, so we opted to enjoy the scenery as we followed the cart path back to the clubhouse. The drive was pleasant, and the homes were beautiful. On our way back, I found one brand-new ball so at the 18th tee, I decided that I would take the final golf swing of my life. I teed the ball up and made what was surely one of the hardest and fastest swings in golf history. The ball exploded off of the club face and sailed about 270 yards straight down the fairway. The waiting foursome applauded and someone yelled, "Wow! What a golf shot." That did it. I was hooked. Over the remainder of our stay, I played two rounds per day. When I got home, I bought a set of Pings and outfitted myself with incredibly flashy golf attire. My wife has never picked up another club. Through the years she has often accompanied me as an observer, though. She applauds when I make par or an exceptionally good shot. She gives me a kiss for each birdie, and two kisses for each eagle. Double kisses are rare enough to be put on the endangered species list.

The Word

Mal. 3:6 – For I am the LORD, I do not change. . . .
Heb. 13:8 – Jesus Christ is the same yesterday, today, and forever.
Lk. 6:19 – And the whole multitude sought to touch Him, for power went out from Him and healed them all.
Jn. 14:16-18,21,23 – And I will pray the Father, and He will give you another Helper, that He may abide with you forever, the Spirit of truth, whom the world cannot receive, because it neither sees Him nor knows Him; but you know Him, for He dwells with you and will be in you. I will not leave you orphans; I will come to you. . . . He who has My commandments and keeps them, it is he who loves Me. And he who loves Me will be loved by My Father, and I will love him and manifest Myself to him. " . . . Jesus answered and said to him, "If anyone loves Me, he will keep My word; and My Father will love him, and We will come to him and make Our home with him."
Acts 4:31 – And when they had prayed, the place where they were assembled together was shaken; and they were all filled with the Holy Spirit, and they spoke the word of God with boldness.
1 Jn. 1:2-3 – The life was manifested, and we have seen, and bear witness, and declare to you that eternal life which was with the Father and was manifested to us, that which we have seen and heard we declare to you, that you also may have fellowship with us; and truly our fellowship is with the Father and with His Son Jesus Christ.

Gleanings From the Word

I was 53 years of age when I experienced physical feelings of the tangible presence of God for the first time. I had been drawn to the Toronto Airport Christian Fellowship in Canada by secular and

3

religious publications, which reported that over a three-year period, 1.5 million Christians had visited this church to experience a visitation of the Holy Spirit.

For two days I observed that, at a certain point during each service, the atmosphere of the sanctuary seemed to be suddenly transformed. It became saturated with the sense that pure love and total acceptance were descending upon each seeker and flooding every aspect of their beings. As this awesome, invigorating force filled the room, people began to experience physiological responses: Some began to laugh joyfully like children who had never known a day of responsibility or emotional stress. Others trembled with what appeared to be spasms from light jolts of heavenly electricity. Many swooned, gently collapsing to the floor as their physical strength melted under the release of holy unconditional love. Most simply sat and soaked in the current of spiritual energy that was pulsating through the room.

On the third day, I had my encounter with the Lord's presence. I was at the back of the meeting hall, looking through the "lost and found." My mind was completely detached from spiritual thoughts. I had once been in the apparel business, and I was curious to examine what types of clothing the visitors had inadvertently left behind. Suddenly, every faculty in my body and mind was flooded with a tingling sensation. I lost all strength and slipped to the floor weeping. I knew that God was touching me, so I did the first religious thing that came to mind: I began to repent. To my amazement, every time I mentioned one of my many blunders, an audible inner voice responded with a statement of appreciation for other things that I had done right. One-half hour later, when I arose from the floor, I was a changed man. From that day till this, I have had numerous encounters with the tangible presence of God.

In my estimation, the Church has been robbed. The primary culprit is Greek philosophy, which has polluted Christian theology

4

for centuries. This ancient philosophy of dualism holds that man's soul (mind) and body are separate entities. It questions the legitimacy of spiritual feelings. It asserts that the only reliable source of knowledge comes solely through the intellect. This insidious error erodes our sacred privilege to know and feel Father God's love through intimate fellowship. When distilled into Christian thinking, it implies that emotional and physical feelings should never be considered as important in our relationship with the Lord. This tainted doctrinal interpretation stands in direct conflict with the Scriptures. They reveal that man was created with the three interrelated capacities of spirit, soul and body. Whatever affects the spirit of a man has the potential to influence his soul and body also.

God does not change. He did take time to come down from heaven to personally enjoy a meal and laughter-filled conversation with His first covenant couple, Abraham and Sarah (Gen. 18:1-15). The pre-incarnate Son of God did appear to Jacob as a man and wrestle with him all night long (Gen. 32:24-30). Surely, if all the Lord wanted to do was cripple Jacob, He could have done so in an instant. However, apparently there is something in the Redeemer that caused Him to long for an opportunity to physically feel the embrace of His creation.

The multitudes that thronged to Jesus did so because they hoped to experience the feelings of His virtue flowing into their lives to heal their sick bodies and wounded souls. Jesus promised that He would not leave us as orphans, but that He would send the Holy Spirit to live in us in the same manner in which Jesus had lived with the 12 apostles. Jesus personally touched them in every way during the three years of His earthly ministry. If we are not experiencing the same type of full fellowship with the Father and the Son through the Holy Spirit, we are living as orphans. It is our biblical heritage as adopted children of God to sense the Lord's presence in our spirits, souls and bodies.

5

Faith's Response

Father, I do not want to live like a spiritual orphan any longer. I have never honestly felt your tangible fatherly affection, but I deeply desire it. In your time, I ask that you will grant me a divine visitation wherein my whole being will be permeated through Your awesome touch.

Chapter Two

YOUR BUILDING PERMIT

A Golf Tip

If you desire to build a sound golf game, it is mandatory that you build on a good foundation. Unlike other sports, golf yields few permits for success to those who insist on being self-taught. When I started, I quickly broke 100, because I had good hand-to-eye coordination. But I played in the miserable high 90s for two years. Then I humbled myself and rented Arnold Palmer's "Basics of Golf" video series. It showed me the proper grip and the best stances and ball placements for wood and iron shots. This technique equipped me to begin to shoot in the high 80s. Your building permit for an enjoyable game is readily available from a good teaching professional or an instructional video series.

The Word

Heb. 6:1-3 – Therefore, leaving the discussion of the elementary principles of Christ, let us go on to perfection, not laying again the foundation of repentance from dead works and of faith toward God, of the doctrine of baptisms, of laying on of hands, of resurrection of the dead, and of eternal judgment. And this we will do if God permits.

Gleanings From the Word

Building a successful Christian life is similar to building a beautiful home: Both require that you secure a building permit. Cities issue permits to ensure that those who build do so according to code. God requires no less, because He loves us too much to chance our building on a faulty foundation. Therefore, He will not permit us to mature unless we are building according to the code of the six foundation doctrines of the Christian faith listed in Hebrews 6:1-3. The following is a cursory outline of these basic truths:

1) **Repentance from dead works**. Repentance means to change your mind and direction 180 degrees. God has never changed His mind about man's need to repent as he turns to Christ. In Acts 2:37-39, the religious Jews asked Peter what they must do to receive Christ. The initial word of his response was *repentance.* The context reveals that it is essential for anyone whom the Lord calls to repent as they turn to Him.

We are to turn from two forms of "dead works." The first is all the sinful acts that we committed when flowing with the spirit of disobedience, as it manipulated the desires of our flesh and minds prior to our knowledge of Christ (Eph. 2:1-3). The second type of dead works from which we need to repent is our attempts to prove ourselves worthy of God's kingdom by any religious act other than faith in Jesus' atoning work of grace on the cross.

2) **Faith toward God**. Our faith is in the Lordship of Jesus as the only begotten Son of God, and in God as our loving heavenly Father. Our faith is walked out by our ongoing confidence in the reliability of the Scriptures as God's Word.

3) **The doctrine of baptisms**. Baptism is in the plural because there are two types. In each, we are immersed into one of two distinct substances, water or the Holy Spirit.

According to Romans 6:3-4, baptism in water is our identification with the death, burial and resurrection of the Lord. It is an

8

outward sign of our inward decision to be separated from our old lifestyle and to live in obedience to the Lord.

The baptism in the Holy Spirit is an event subsequent to one's salvation in which we are filled with the Holy Spirit and empowered with spiritual gifts to assist us in our Christian lives. This experience is not the same as receiving the Holy Spirit in the new birth. In Acts 8, the people who had been evangelized and baptized in water under the preaching of Philip later received the infilling of the Spirit through the ministry of Peter and John.

In water baptism, we are immersed in water by a servant of the Lord. With the baptism of the Holy Spirit, Jesus baptizes us in the Spirit to enable us to demonstrate power as His servants (Jn. 1:33).

4) **Laying on of hands**. We lay hands on people to impart the Holy Spirit and physical healing (Mk. 16:17-18 and Acts 19:6) Through the laying on of hands, both spiritual gifts and authority are transmitted from one believer to another (1 Tim. 4:14).

5) **Resurrection of the dead**. There are two, the first of which is called the first resurrection, which has two phases. According to 1 Thessalonians 4:16-17, phase one will take place at the rapture. Phase two will take place prior to the 1,000-year reign of Christ (Rev. 20:4-6). The second resurrection will happen after the millennium. This is the time at which all those who have not been resurrected previously will come back to life (Rev. 20:7-15).

6) **The eternal judgment.** There are three judgment seats at which different categories of people will be judged to determine their various rewards or eternal destinies. At the judgment seat of Christ, believers will be judged to determine their rewards in the hereafter (2 Cor. 5:10). At the throne of Christ's glory, nations will be assessed as to how they treated the Lord's brothers. His natural brothers are the Jewish people, and His spiritual brothers are Christians (Mt. 25:31-46). The final judgment takes place after the millennium at the great white throne. There, all those who did not know the Lord will be judged to determine their eternal destiny (Rev. 20:11-15).

Faith's Response

Lord, I want to mature in my walk with you. I will imitate the Christians of Berea by exploring the Scriptures daily to see if these things are so (Acts 17:10-11).

Chapter Three
HE TRAINS MY HANDS
A Golf Tip

A proper grip is essential for a good golf swing and satisfying shots. Here, in six steps, is a reasonable way to ensure a correct grip:

1) Build your stance around the club head after it has been placed behind the ball, with the sweet spot aiming toward the intended target.

2) If you are right-handed, reach out and "shake hands" with the club, using your left hand. The portion of your palm nearest your wrist should be at least one inch below the top of the shaft handle. The crease between your index finger and thumb needs to point toward your right shoulder.

3) Now "shake hands" with the club, using your right hand. Interlock the little finger of your right hand with the index finger of your left hand. The crease between the index finger and thumb of your right hand should be pointing toward your right shoulder.

4) If your have trouble with a slice, lightly twist your left and right hands inwardly towards one another. This slight adjustment will prevent your right elbow from coming out too much from your body during your swing.

5) As you stand over the ball, your shoulders, arms and hands should form an upside-down triangle. Your shoulders represent the short side of the triangle, and your arms form the "V" of the triangle.

6) You can train your hands to automatically take the correct grip. Practice taking the proper grip while watching television. Should you practice while reprimanding your children, I can assure you that you will have their undivided attention.

The Word

Ps. 144:1 – Blessed be the Lord my Rock, who trains my hands for war, and my fingers for battle.

1 Pet. 5:8-9 – Be sober, be vigilant; because your adversary the devil walks about like a roaring lion, seeking whom he may devour. Resist him, steadfast in the faith, knowing that the same sufferings are experienced by your brotherhood in the world.

Eph. 6:12 – For we do not wrestle against flesh and blood, but against principalities, against powers, against the rulers of the darkness of this age, against spiritual hosts of wickedness in the heavenly places.

Rev. 12:10-11 – Then I heard a loud voice saying in heaven, "Now salvation, and strength, and the kingdom of our God, and the power of His Christ have come, for the accuser of our brethren, who accused them before our God day and night, has been cast down. And they overcame him by the blood of the Lamb and by the word of their testimony, and they did not love their lives to the death."

Gleanings From the Word

Every day we encounter situations which are covertly influenced by Satan's invisible forces of darkness. He goes about as a hungry lion preying upon human weakness and naïveté. Though we cannot see the lion, we can easily discern the evidence of his presence. His roar is heard through the screams of frustrated anger as parents batter the self-esteem of their children. Marriages fall apart as the force of his blows exaggerates the character faults of the partners one to another. Teenagers run away from home in the grip of his jaws of rebellion. Hospitals are filled with those who have been raked with the claws of his wasting diseases. And we see his droppings in the pornography which litters our culture.

God has not abandoned us to continually have our lives altered by negative influences from the spiritual realm. His Word equips us with the understanding of the source of many of life's perplexities. Our flesh is not the primary source of our difficulties. Our major battle is with the demonic spirits of wickedness that are subtly motivating the thoughts and actions of people. The Scriptures teach us that, in order to overcome these spiritual forces, we must use spiritual weapons. Our physical strength is to no avail, as we cannot grapple with these powers with our hands, but He does train our spiritual hands to use the spiritual weapons of the gifts of the Spirit. Satanic powers flee when we touch troublesome people with compassionate hands that are anointed by the Holy Spirit.

We also can pull down the powers of darkness with the words of our testimonies concerning the authority of the blood of the Lamb. Satan is rendered helpless when we war against him in prayer, confessing what the Bible says the blood of Jesus has accomplished for us. The following is a very effective confession based on Scripture.

Through the blood of Jesus, all of my sins have been forgiven. Therefore, Satan has no power over me and no unsettled claims against me. My body is the temple of the Holy Spirit, redeemed, cleansed and made holy by the blood of Jesus. My body is for the Lord, and the Lord is for my body. Because of the power of God's blood, my physical members are instruments of righteousness yielded to God for His glory and His service. Through the authority of Jesus' name and the power of His blood, I now command every demonic spirit to cease and desist your assignments against me and those I care for. Satan, your influence over our minds, actions and circumstances is hereby canceled by the blood of Jesus.

Faith's Response

Vocalize this confession in your prayers. Interject the names of people and situations wherever you discern that Satan has been exercising illegal influence.

Chapter Four

HIGH ANXIETY

A Golf Tip

X (Playing With Strangers)/ Y (No Warm Up)

+ Z (The First Tee)

$= A^2$ (High Anxiety)

When playing with strangers, the first tee can be one of the most terrifying places on the planet. Your customary first hole "jitters" can mutate into high anxiety unless you take some mental and physical precautions:

1) Try to hit some warm-up balls so your body will be limber enough to allow you to hit a good first shot.

2) Realize that the other players are most likely going through the same thing that you are. To them you may look like a scratch player.

3) Tee off with the club in which you have the most confidence. A decent 175-yard five iron shot is far less embarrassing and costly than an out-of-bounds slice.

The Word

Prov. 19:23 – The fear of the Lord leads to life, and he who has it will abide in satisfaction; he will not be visited with evil.

Deut. 28:65-67 – And among those nations you shall find no rest, nor shall the sole of your foot have a resting place; but there the Lord will give you a trembling heart, failing eyes, and anguish of soul. Your life shall hang in doubt before you; you shall fear day and night, and have no assurance of life. In the morning you shall say, 'Oh, that it were evening!' And at evening you shall say, 'Oh, that it were morning!' because of the fear which terrifies your heart.

2 Tim. 1:7 – For God has not given us a spirit of fear, but of power and of love and of a sound mind.

Rom. 8:15 – For you did not receive the spirit of bondage again to fear, but you received the Spirit of adoption by whom we cry out, "Abba, Father."

Philip. 4:6-7 – Be anxious for nothing, but in everything by prayer and supplication, with thanksgiving, let your requests be made known to God; and the peace of God, which surpasses all understanding, will guard your hearts and minds through Christ Jesus.

1 Jn. 4:18 – There is no fear in love; but perfect love casts out fear, because fear involves torment. But he who fears has not been made perfect in love.

Gleanings From the Word

No one can live entirely free of fear. There are both positive and negative types of fear. God has designed us emotionally and spiritually in such a way that we would be incomplete without the capacity for some elements of positive fear. The ability to feel fear is as necessary as peripheral vision. Wholesome natural apprehension cautions us from reckless driving. A respectful fear which is interwoven with our love for our marriage partner restrains us from saying or doing things which might jeopardize our relationship with them. The most strategic fear which we can cultivate is the reverential fear of the Lord. It has many rewards. If we have it, we will be granted long, satisfying lives. It even thwarts the forces of evil in their attempts to visit us.

Without a doubt, our generation is suffering from high anxiety because we have attempted to exempt ourselves from our mandatory portion of the fear of God. There is a severe penalty for not embracing this positive aspect of fear. The vacuum which its absence leaves in our hearts can attract multiple negative, enslaving fears. We then can become overwhelmed with the fear of man and the impending dread of some catastrophic event that might befall us in the near future. Our hearts tremble with concern about financial ruin, the possible loss of a child, or the thoughts of a devastating illness striking us.

When these types of fears plague us, they are not initiated by the hand of God. Satan discerns our lack of security because we do not walk in the fear of the Lord. He fills the vacancy with diverse manifestations of the spirit of fear. However, God does not abandon us to fend for ourselves as hapless victims of perpetual anxiety attacks. There is always a remedy through Christ.

First, we must humble ourselves and acknowledge the reality of our fears to God in prayer. Many of the Psalms are King David's confessions of fear to his loving heavenly Father, whom he knew possessed the balm which could alleviate every fear. Then, we should offer thanksgiving to God for being our affectionate Abba God (loving Father God). As we do this, we must exercise our faith to trust that He is sending His love to settle down around us and in us. The presence of His love casts out all fear. Once the assurance of the love of God makes its nest in our hearts, the peace of God will reign supreme in our formally troubled minds.

$$L \text{ (Love Of God)} / A \text{ (Your Anxiety)}$$

$$+ T \text{ (Prayers of Thanksgiving)}$$

$$= P^{10} \text{ (Peace That Passes Understanding)}$$

Faith's Response

Heavenly Father, I confess that my heart is filled with many types of fear. My anxiety level is high because I have entertained an exaggerated confidence in my own strength to make it in this world. Father God, I thank You for loving me. I believe that You are flooding me now with wave after wave of the assurance of Your loving care. I praise Your name that You are vanquishing my fears and instilling the reign of Your peace in my heart and mind.

Chapter Five

HEAVEN ON THE LINKS

A Golf Story

David Yonggi Cho is the founding pastor of the 750,000 member Full Gospel Central Church of Seoul, Korea. This dynamic man of faith is also an avid golfer. Several years ago, he was playing with my good friend, Quentin Edwards, and he said two rather humorous things. After 17 holes, they were tied. Cho had already putted out for a five, and it was Quentin's turn to putt for a four. Cho interrupted him by removing his hat and praying loudly: "Hebenly Faza, I ask you to gib my bruda Quenchen a good putt." When Quentin made his putt and won the match, Cho sighed, removed his hat again, bowed his head and prayed: "Faza, I did not mean fo you to gib him good enough putt to beat me." Later, he said to Edwards; "Quenchen, you are six days oder dan me. It is your responsibility to die and go to heben fust, and make sure dat Jesus has built my mansion on berry nice golf course. If it is not on golf course, you must see to its relocation." Personally, I have put in my request for my mansion to be built on the left side of a par three fairway near the tee box. I want protection from heavenly slicers.

The Word

Deut. 11:18-19,21 – "Therefore you shall lay up these words of mine in your heart and in your soul, and bind them as a sign on your hand, and they shall be as frontlets between your eyes. You shall teach them to your children, speaking of them when you sit in your house, when you walk by the way, when you lie down, and when you rise up. . . . that your days and the days of your children may be multiplied in the land of which the Lord swore to your fathers to give them, like the days of the heavens above the earth.

Rev. 21:1,3-4 – Now I saw a new heaven and a new earth, for the first heaven and the first earth had passed away. Also there was no more sea. . . . And I heard a loud voice from heaven saying, "Behold, the tabernacle of God is with men, and He will dwell with them, and they shall be His people. God Himself will be with them and be their God. And God will wipe away every tear from their eyes; there shall be no more death, nor sorrow, nor crying. There shall be no more pain, for the former things have passed away."

Titus 2:13 – . . . looking for the blessed hope and glorious appearing of our great God and Savior Jesus Christ.

1 Cor. 15:51-52 – Behold, I tell you a mystery: We shall not all sleep, but we shall all be changed in a moment, in the twinkling of an eye, at the last trumpet. For the trumpet will sound, and the dead will be raised incorruptible, and we shall be changed.

Gleanings From the Word

Practically every Christian golfer with whom I have golfed mentions the possibility of golf in heaven. When I am having a good round, I enjoy discussing the prospects of continuing to cultivate my prowess on the links in the hereafter. On the occasions when my game is not at its best, I dismiss all thoughts of golf in heaven with a less than enthusiastic response: "It is doubtful that there will be golf in heaven for two reasons. First of all, if there was golf there, it wouldn't be heaven—it would be hell! Secondly, the Scripture teaches that in heaven there will be no more sorrow, crying or tears. Where there is golf, you inevitably will find all three." If I happen to hit several nice shots after this gloomy retort, I hasten to follow it with: "However, on the other hand, during the millennium there will most likely be opportunities for us to continue enjoying this challenging sport here on earth. We Christians will have glorified bodies, like the Lord, and will therefore have sub-par handicaps. Anyone living at the time of the rapture who is not a Christian will enter the 1,000-year reign of Christ without a glorified body. This means we Christian golfers will be able to mystify and defeat non-Christian touring pros."

Even if there is no golf in heaven, we can have "heaven on the links" in the here-and-now. If we give ourselves to making the Word of God a priority in our daily living, the days of our lives can be like the days of heaven on earth. God honors meditation on His Word to the extent that He graces those who meditate with the ability to regularly taste the joys of heaven before the hereafter. If we give the Word prominence, it will usher in heavenly righteousness, peace and joy to our home-lives and our vocations, as well as to our leisure time on the golf links.

The Scriptures imply that our existence in heaven will encompass far more than leisure time in endless duration. One of the redemptive names of the Lord is *Jehovah Elohim,* which means "the Lord, the eternal Creator." Our God is a God of divine productive activity. In the beginning, He worked six days, then rested on the Sabbath. Jesus and the Holy Spirit both dwell in the eternal realm, yet they are active. Jesus continually makes intercession for His Body on earth. The Holy Spirit has been entrusted with the delegated authority of the Father and the Son. He is presently occupied as the divine administrator of truth and blessing to the Church on behalf of the Godhead. The holy angels are constantly ministering to those who are, or will become, the heirs of salvation. Though

Moses and Elijah passed into eternity years before the time of Jesus, they played an active part in His transfiguration. The apostles saw them speaking to Jesus about things concerning His impending death. In heaven, God, His angels and the departed believers who have gone on before us are all productively occupied with important tasks. Therefore, it appears that we would feel very awkward in heaven if all we did was play golf and float about on clouds.

God created us in His own image for His eternal purposes. In heaven, we will be occupied with pursuits which complement God's creative attributes. The event of the rapture is called the blessed hope, because it is to eclipse every other good hope in the hearts and minds of God's people. If we give the hope of His return priority over all our other hopes and pursuits, He will make the days of our lives like the days of heaven upon earth.

Faith's Response

Father, I thank you for the hope that You have put within me to perform with excellence in all of my vocational and leisurely pursuits here on earth. But Lord, I confess unto you that they all pale when compared to the exhilaration which I feel at the thought of the blessed hope of Your return. Come quickly, Lord Jesus.

Chapter Six

"NICE WORK, LORD!"

A Golf Story

Westchester Country Club does not have a cart girl to sell snacks to the golfers while they are playing, but a scantily clad "Delilah" does come by and set up shop on a public road that parallels the eighth hole. Golfers go out of their way just to see her, so one could say that her marketing approach was successful from a certain point of view.

On one occasion, I myself needed to do something to subdue my own lustful thoughts and also distract the attention of the trio of golfers I had just joined, so that they would not fall prey to temptation as well. At that moment, I remembered that we are to praise the Lord for all things. So I loudly called out, "Thank you, Lord, for all the beautiful handiwork of your creation. And when it comes to Your daughter there, I want to congratulate You, too: Nice work, Lord! Let me see her and treat her the way You do."

At this, my playing partners chuckled. Having been subtly reminded that I was a clergyman and that they had daughters of their own, they resumed play without further comment.

The Word

Heb. 4:15 – For we do not have a High Priest who cannot sympathize with our weaknesses, but was in all points tempted as we are, yet without sin.

Mt. 5:27-28 – "You have heard that it was said to those of old, 'You shall not commit adultery.' But I say to you that whoever looks at a woman to lust for her has already committed adultery with her in his heart."

1 Cor. 6:13,15-19 – Foods for the stomach and the stomach for foods, but God will destroy both it and them. Now the body is not for sexual immorality but for the Lord, and the Lord for the body.... Do you not know that your bodies are members of Christ? Shall I then take the members of Christ and make them members of a harlot? Certainly not! Or do you not know that he who is joined to a harlot is one body with her? For "the two," He says, "shall become one flesh." But he who is joined to the Lord is one spirit with Him. Flee sexual immorality. Every sin that a man does is outside the body, but he who commits sexual immorality sins against his own body. Or do you not know that your body is the temple of the Holy Spirit who is in you, whom you have from God, and you are not your own?

Job 31:1 – I made a covenant with mine eyes; why then should I think upon a maid? (KJV)

James 5:16 – Confess your faults one to another, and pray one for another, that ye may be healed. The effectual fervent prayer of a righteous man availeth much (KJV).

Gleanings From the Word

Perhaps the most frequent prayer request that I encounter when counseling men is for help with the problem of lust. I always try to encourage them that they are not alone in their temptations. Every man who has ever lived, including the Lord Jesus, has been confronted with this issue. That's right, even the Lord was tempted with spontaneous, uninvited sexual thoughts. Here on earth, He did not breeze through on His Deity. He made it as a man who was tempted like we are, but was unique in that He

24

never let the temptations progress into sins. Surely He was God, but He was also fully a man. He was equipped with the same hormone levels and the risk of possible temptation that all healthy men experience. He can empathize with the feelings of our temptations because He, too, experienced them.

Though it is not sinful to experience the sensation of temptation, it is sinful to entertain lustful thoughts. In God's eyes, to look on a woman with lingering lust is one and the same as committing the physical act. Jesus is so committed to us that He does not abandon us, including when we are in the midst of sin. The Lord actually allows us to drag Him through the mire of our lustful thoughts and acts. He, of course, does not condone our actions, and He most definitely makes His presence known. The pain of guilt registers in our consciences and prevents us from truly enjoying sin's folly.

Our bodies and minds were not created to be continually overpowered by lust. Our bodies are for the Lord. We are not our own, for we have been washed and made holy for the Lord in the name of Jesus and by the Spirit of God.

Here are three steps one can take to alleviate lustful thoughts:

1) Take the position that you have no option to allow thoughts to linger which dishonor the Lord. We have no spiritual right to entertain thoughts that we cannot legally fulfill. Therefore, make a covenant with your eyes that you will not stare at any woman in a manner that could provoke lust.

2) Defuse the scandal of the event by using it as a prompting to pray that God bless the person who occasions your lust. This initiative usually causes the thoughts to diminish.

3) If the thoughts become habitual, confess them to an honorable person who knows how to pray. Personally, I confess them to my wife Prudence. The accountability factor, along with her threatening smile as she quotes her favorite Scripture verse, evaporates the problem for months on end. "A man who wanders from the

way of understanding [prudence] will rest in the assembly of the dead" (Prov. 21:16).

Faith's Response

Father, forgive me for dragging your Son through the mire of my lustful thoughts. I hereby make a covenant with You and my eyes, that I will not look on anything which could awaken lust within me.

Chapter Seven

WHAT YOU SAY
IS WHAT YOU GET

A Golf Tip

Nearly all golfers are suspect of neurotic or paranoid tendencies. We talk to golf balls in flight: "Come in, baby . . . Now cut—I said, cut! . . . No, no, no. That's right, you backsliding heifer: Do it to me again . . . Go ahead and run into the water. I knew you would do it to me." Speaking to a golf ball, as psychotic as it may appear, is actually not an unfounded practice. It's all in the timing. After it is in flight, it's too late. All of your energy has already committed it to a given path. The time to start your instructions is on your way from the last green to the next tee box. Your pep talk should continue through your ball strike. "Okay, Mr. Ultra, I'm going to send you out on this 150 yard, par three with my seven iron. You are going to come off the sweet spot of the club, head high and pretty. Then you are going to fade over that tree and the left sand trap, onto the green, two feet from the pin. Did you hear me? Now, let us go through it again." As you do this, your mind will program your body to execute your commands.

The Word

Mk. 11:22-24 – So Jesus answered and said to them, "Have faith in God. For assuredly, I say to you, whoever says to this mountain,

'Be removed and be cast into the sea,' and does not doubt in his heart, but believes that those things he says will be done, he will have whatever he says. Therefore I say to you, whatever things you ask when you pray, believe that you receive them, and you will have them."

Rom. 4:17 – (as it is written, "I have made you a father of many nations") in the presence of Him whom he believed—God, who gives life to the dead and calls those things which do not exist as though they did.

Gleanings From the Word

Faith speaks! When you are seeking to apprehend a spiritual or material blessing from God, a sound scriptural strategy is to continually speak forth that you have possession of it, even before you actually request it in prayer. As you frequently declare that you have the provision, the intensity of faith in your heart is increased and established to the extent that you will know the desired blessing is already yours, in the Spirit, when you do pray for it. The more that you say it before you pray, it the more likely it will be that you will receive it after you have prayed for it.

God Himself speaks of things that do not yet exist as though they did. He instructed Abraham to follow suit when He changed his name from Abram to Abraham. Abraham means "the father of multitudes of nations." Years before he had any children, he was introducing himself to everyone he met as the father of multitudes of nations. Each introduction was a faith declaration of something that was real in the spiritual realm because God had promised it. However, the miracle had not yet occurred in the temporal realm. By the time he was 100 years old, his faith was so established in his heart that Sarah conceived Isaac. After that, miracle after miracle took place, as he fathered many other children when he was well past 110.

Mark 11:22-24 encourages us to have faith in God by speaking to the obstacles that are hindering our path in life. If you are an observant traveler, you don't wait until you are at the foot of the mountain before making plans as to how you are to travel around it. You will see the mountain from afar and begin to speak about what path you should take so that the mountain will not be an obstacle. Why climb over it or take the time to go around the problem? God says you can speak to the hindrance, and it will vanish, if you believe that it will in your heart.

The Greek word for salvation means more than grace for eternal life. It means healing, deliverance, preservation, wholeness and safety. With our mouths, we make a confession that brings us into the form of salvation we are seeking. If we are temporarily out of money, we declare that God has supplied all of our needs according to His riches in glory. The verbal speaking of this promise builds faith in our hearts, so that we will know that God hears us when we do pray about our finances.

How do you believe that you have received something when you pray for it, prior to its actual materialization in the temporal realm? Consider this example: You have ordered a new driver from a TV offer. They have your credit card number. You believe that they are a reliable firm, and they have said it will take five days for delivery. Before the club ever arrives, you are enjoying it. You tell your buddies about your new driver. You can see yourself hitting it marvelously before it is in your physical possession. You have received the club in your heart and mind and thoroughly enjoy it, because you know that everything needed to make it appear has been activated. God is far more reliable than any golf firm, and His promises are more sure. Speak about your needed provision as already provided and enjoy it before you see it, and you will have it.

Faith's Response

Spiritual:

You have a wayward daughter. You speak of her in this way. "God is calling our daughter to Himself. She knows the reality of the love of the Lord in her heart of hearts. Soon, we will see her giving her testimony to all of her friends." Your prayer could be, "Lord, I thank You for saving Mary. I am so happy that she is giving her life to You. Lord Jesus, I know she is very safe in Your hands."

Material:

You need a new car. You speak to your family about the new car you are believing for, describing its model, color and accessories, saying, "The Lord is giving us a new, fully loaded Buick 'Park Avenue.' It is the most gorgeous emerald green." Your prayer could be, "Lord, I'm so grateful for our new car. I praise you for blessing us with our beautiful Park Avenue."

Chapter Eight
WHAT YOU SEE IS
WHAT YOU GET

A Golf Tip

To make a good golf shot, it is essential that you discipline
yourself to visualize the shot before you make it. Your body will do
its best to follow the thought picture you have instilled within your
mind. Envision your set up, back swing, and where your club will
hit the ball as you follow through to complete the swing. Play an
inner motion picture of the ball's flight path and landing at a specific target.

The Word

Prov. 29:18 – Where there is no vision, the people perish.
Acts 2:17 – "And it shall come to pass in the last days," says God,
"That I will pour out of My Spirit on all flesh; your sons and your
daughters shall prophesy, your young men shall see visions, your
old men shall dream dreams."
Jn. 1:48-51 – Nathanael said to Him, "How do You know me?"
Jesus answered and said to him, "Before Philip called you, when
you were under the fig tree, I saw you." Nathanael answered and
said to Him, "Rabbi, You are the Son of God! You are the King of
Israel!" Jesus answered and said to him, "Because I said to you, 'I

saw you under the fig tree,' do you believe? You will see greater things than these." And He said to him, "Most assuredly, I say to you, hereafter you shall see heaven open, and the angels of God ascending and descending upon the Son of Man."

Gleanings From the Word

The term "vision" carries many definitions and implications for the contemporary Christian. In the secular realm, it can mean dynamic aspirations for the future. The Scriptures imply that there are several different types. First, there are Spirit-inspired thought pictures that come spontaneously when one is fully awake. Next are spiritual dreams, visions in which God speaks to His servants when they are asleep. Most of the prophetic books of the Bible came to their authors in the form of visions. They wrote down and proclaimed verbally what they had seen in their visions.

The third type of biblical visions could be called creative visions. This is where the believer uses his own initiative as a paintbrush that is dipped into his understanding of the Word of God and the Lord's revealed will for his life. He then paints a visualization of his perception of God's highest will for a specific situation on the canvas of his imagination. He holds on to this thought picture in faith until what he sees in the inner realm is duplicated in his temporal circumstances.

The Psalms are resplendent with examples of David's creative visualizations. In Psalms 91:4, his meditation was that he could find refuge under the feathers of the Lord's wings. God is not a big bird. Created in God's image, we do not have feathers because neither does He. In Psalms 52:8, David envisioned himself like a green olive tree flourishing in the house of the Lord. The symbols of the feathered wings and the olive tree that he painted on the canvas of his imagination helped David build his faith to flow in the protection and righteousness of God.

Unfortunately, many sincere Christians have avoided visions for fear of entanglement with the "New Age." The New Age brand of creative visualization is at best limited, as its source is exaggerated confidence in the power of the human mind. Christian creative visions are far different. Our faith is not in the creative power of our thoughts, rather in the faithfulness of the Almighty Creator to respond to our faith visualizations of His person and Word for our good.

Satanic mimicry should never thwart the exploration of legitimate scriptural tools. Moses fearlessly continued in faith when the magicians of Pharaoh duplicated the first three signs that God had commissioned him to perform (Ex. 7-8). They duplicated turning rods into serpents, water into blood, and the plague of frogs. Moses continued in faith until he did something they could not do—specifically, changing the dust into lice.

Jesus called visions great things. When Nathanael marveled that Jesus had seen him through a vision sitting under the fig tree, the Master's response was to assure him that he, too, would receive them in the future. We need both an overall vision and individual visions to apprehend the will of the Lord for our generation. Without them, our hopes will perish into mediocrity. Our arsenal of faith is incomplete unless we utilize Bible-based creative visualization. We should decorate the inner rooms of our hearts and minds with Spirit-inspired thought pictures of God's highest will for our ministries, families and vocations. Then we should hold on in faith until we see them materialize in our circumstances.

Faith's Response

Lord, I desire every good and perfect gift that you have for me. I ask you to open the eyes of my heart for visions from you. Lord, thank You for the courage to paint images of Your will on the canvas of my imagination and the faith to see them realized.

Chapter Nine
THE DIVINE NINE

A Golf Tip

Callaway's "Divine Nine" metal wood is a great utility club for a 145-165 yard shot into the wind or from a troublesome lie. The sixth hole of a course I frequently play is a 375 yard par four. A wide stream runs across the fairway 30 yards from its elevated green, which is surrounded by bunkers. My approach shot is normally around 160 yards into a head wind. My "Divine Nine" has put me in the position for birdies on many occasions.

The Word

1 Cor. 12:1,7-10 – Now concerning spiritual gifts, brethren, I do not want you to be ignorant. . . . But the manifestation of the Spirit is given to each one for the profit of all: for to one is given the word of wisdom through the Spirit, to another the word of knowledge through the same Spirit, to another faith by the same Spirit, to another gifts of healings by the same Spirit, to another the working of miracles, to another prophecy, to another discerning of spirits, to another different kinds of tongues, to another the interpretation of tongues.

1 Pet. 4:10 – As each one has received a gift, minister it to one another, as good stewards of the manifold grace of God.

Gleanings From the Word

Every believer has been given access to spiritual gifts with which we are to minister one to another. I call the nine congregational gifts mentioned in 1 Corinthians 12:7-10, "The Divine Nine." These spiritual gifts can be divided into three groups. The first three gifts *say* something: prophecy, tongues and the interpretation of tongues. The second three *do* something: the gift of faith, healing, and the working of miracles. The final three *reveal* something: a word of wisdom, a word of knowledge, and the discerning of spirits.

Prophecy is a divinely inspired proclamation that brings forth edifying awareness of God's love and future plans for people. The type of tongues cited in this passage is a spontaneous public utterance in a language unknown to the speaker. Through the subsequent gift of interpretation, the gift of tongues serves essentially the same purpose as prophecy. The gift of faith gives one the courage and ability to accomplish exploits for God that would be unthinkable in our own strength. The gifts of healing accelerate the body's God-given healing propensity to an instantaneous mode. The workings of miracles brings about the restoration of health to a body organ or member which could not be affected through medicine or the natural healing processes. A word of knowledge reveals facts that need to be known. The word of wisdom gives understanding of how to do something in a manner outside one's normal limitations. The discernings of spirits gives revelation relating to the activity of invisible spirit beings.

God never gives gifts without purpose. Our own abilities, education and experience are too limited to enable us to represent the Lord as His Body. The Church must have the assistance of "The Divine Nine"—the gifts of the Spirit—to demonstrate God's power to the world.

Faith's Response

Lord, I thank You for all my natural talents. But they are inadequate to express Your love and power to my contemporaries: Disciple me by Your Spirit so I can flow in Your divine giftings.

Chapter Ten

REGRIPPED

A Golf Tip

If you play more than once per week and have a nominal practice schedule, you should have your clubs regripped every year. Slick grips can cause you to inadvertently hold the club tighter. This increases the potential for pulls, slices and fat shots.

An occasion in which you might need to consider another type of regripping is when you find that you are uncomfortable after you have taken your stance and are prepared to hit. Golf is a mental game, and therefore it is essential that you feel comfortable mentally and physically before hitting. If you sense inner uneasiness, or if the club head looks too open or closed, step back. Then repeat your whole set-up routine and take a new grip. This approach will help lower your potential for bad shots.

The Word

Mt. 18:19-20 – "Again I say to you that if two of you agree on earth concerning anything that they ask, it will be done for them by My Father in heaven. For where two or three are gathered together in My name, I am there in the midst of them."

1 Pet. 3:1 – Wives, likewise, be submissive to your own husbands, that even if some do not obey the word, they, without a word, may be won by the conduct of their wives.

Gleanings From the Word

I was raised in a Christ-centered evangelical home. I was dedicated to the Lord's service from my birth and was born-again at an early age. At age five, I really enjoyed holding my little New Testament and imitating the "fire and brimstone," "God will getcha" preaching which I heard on Sundays. My parents sent me to the finest of Christian secondary schools and colleges. However, during my teen years, I discovered that the flavor of Christianity in which I was brought up lacked essential ingredients: namely, fun, freedom and teaching that cultivates a successful life. To me it seemed that the Church emphasized far more what I *could not* do if I was committed to Christ, as opposed to all that I *could* do through Christ. Having deduced that the aggressive pursuit of Christianity and an enjoyable life were mutually exclusive, I shook off the restraints of legalism. I was not about to have my zest for life and success stifled by an excessive emphasis on keeping the letter of the law, neglecting the far more important spirit of the law.

The Lord knows those who are His own. He had His secret agenda to see to it that I would be "regripped" for His purposes. I married a Christian girl named Prudence. She is well named, as she was very wise in her efforts to see me come back to the Lord. Because of my aversion to church, we did not attend one, and I discouraged her from taking the children in my absence. I would throw wild parties at our home, which in some cases lasted for days. She was a most cordial hostess. She never once protested. She cheerfully served the drinks and cleaned up after everyone. As far as I knew, she had no active interest in the things of the Lord.

On July 18, 1967, I was on a business trip to Tennessee. That night, I began to wonder just how Israel was able to defeat their Moslem neighbors in the Six Day War. Remembering Bible stories from my youth, I knew that God had a special relationship with the Jewish people, and therefore I suspected that they may have had divine assistance. Out of curiosity, I began to read the Bible placed in my room by the Gideons. After reading for a while, I began to have this strange sensation that God knew me and was reading me. I went to light a cigarette, and as I brushed my cheek, I felt a tear. This shocked me for I felt no emotion, and to my knowledge, was certainly not in need of God. I was crisis-free, both emotionally and financially. In response to the surprising tear, I thought it might be appropriate to pray. So I slipped down on my knees for the first time in years. When my knees hit the floor, the fountains of the deep broke forth. I began to wail from the depth of my spirit. Then, I heard myself crying out to God, telling Him that I needed Him, and if He wanted me, I was His man.

When I arrived home, I promptly told Prudence of my experience and authoritatively announced that we would take the children to church on Sunday. She began to laugh and cry simultaneously. She then told me that she, my parents and a local pastor had been agreeing in prayer concerning my backslidden condition.

Certainly my salvation would have been delayed had she attempted the classic "Christian wife's tactics," such as placing Bibles in the bathroom, pastors "happening to drop by" the house, and verbal condemnation concerning my "good-time Charlie" lifestyle. These attempts would have only incited further rebellion. It was her quiet, unobtrusive faith and secret prayers of agreement that brought me to the throne.

Faith's Response

Lord help me to impress others with the joyous freedom of life in You rather than the restrictions of my particular church. May my prayers of agreement with my companions in the faith bring many to the revelation of Your mercy.

Chapter Eleven

LEGALISM OR "A LIFE"

A Golf Tip

Though I am an evangelical clergyman, I have no problem betting on myself in a round of golf. I think it is helpful, rather than sinful. To date, I have found no explicit Scripture references which even remotely imply that small wagers are to be forbidden among people of sincere faith. At this juncture, many can cite horror stories of lives ruined through addiction to gambling. I wholeheartedly concur. Excess in even the most legitimate pleasures can be destructive. Could it be that if the statistics were tallied, there would be far more Christians whose health has been compromised through gluttony than there are gamblers whom have been bankrupted? Moderation is the biblical key. When stakes are kept in the neighborhood of what one would normally spend on other entertainment, there need be no concern for harm. When golfers give strokes to weaker players in hole-by-hole match play, seldom is there meaningful money exchanged.

I propose that betting is helpful, simply because it heightens the intensity of the players' concentration. The amount of the wager is immaterial. It is my observation that most golfers play better when every stroke is made with a tangible goal for winning. Most play as hard for a dime per hole as they do for a dollar per hole. If you want to improve your game, put a little money on your next round. If you lose, you are invited to come down and play with me for the same stakes.

The Word

Col. 2:20-23 – Therefore, if you died with Christ from the basic principles of the world, why, as though living in the world, do you subject yourselves to regulations? "Do not touch, do not taste, do not handle," which all concern things which perish with the using—according to the commandments and doctrines of men? These things indeed have an appearance of wisdom in self-imposed religion, false humility, and neglect of the body, but are of no value against the indulgence of the flesh.

Rom. 14:2-6 – For one believes he may eat all things, but he who is weak eats only vegetables. Let not him who eats despise him who does not eat, and let not him who does not eat judge him who eats; for God has received him. Who are you to judge another's servant? To his own master he stands or falls. Indeed, he will be made to stand, for God is able to make him stand. One person esteems one day above another; another esteems every day alike. Let each be fully convinced in his own mind. He who observes the day, observes it to the Lord; and he who does not observe the day, to the Lord he does not observe it. He who eats, eats to the Lord, for he gives God thanks; and he who does not eat, to the Lord he does not eat, and gives God thanks.

Gleanings From the Word

I was raised in a good Christian home and was sent to the finest Christian schools available. Our lives revolved around church and fellowship with believers. I was saved, and honored the Bible as God's inspired Word. However, it was my observation that most Christian groups seemed to put a far higher premium on compliance to their brand of religious regulations than they did on productive faith. This led me to conclude that I needed to make a choice between two things which I thought were mutually exclusive: I could embrace legalism or have "a life." So I chose to have a life. The day that I left my Free Methodist college at age 21 was the day I left the church. The prospect of spending one more moment in the conservative Christian environment was unattractive.

There is one term that defines my reason for departure from the Church: legalism. It is the cruel two-edged sword of hyper-religiosity. With one edge, it cuts into the souls of Christians who live in fear of breaking a taboo of their sect. Those deemed faithful tend to relate to God and to one another on the basis of agreement about what should be forbidden as opposed to what they can do through Christ and the encouragement of their church. The other edge discourages the unconverted from looking to Christianity as a viable source of truth and comfort. The world has already loaded them with condemnation for their ineptness. Why should they want to expose themselves to religious institutions that openly criticize those within and without, who do not meet their standards? Many sinners would welcome an invitation to have the Lord come into their lives and reshape their values. However, they are not attracted by the prospect of having to jump through spiritual hoops in order to be accepted.

Biblical Christianity is not a religion which puts a priority on rules and regulations. It is a religion which emphasizes harmonious relationships with our fellow man through our submission to the lordship of Jesus. Within the faith, there are few absolutes and many variables in relation to rules about how our faith is to be expressed. Love, faith, knowing the voice of God, regular fellowship, and marital fidelity are absolutes. *When* one prays, *where* one fellowships, *how* one is baptized, *what* one prefers to eat and drink, and *which* earthly enjoyments one can legitimately choose to enjoy are variables. A tragedy of contemporary Christianity is that each sect *majors* on their rules concerning the variables and *minors* on the power of the absolutes.

The passage cited from Romans 14 in today's reading illustrates this point. In verse two, it indicates that one who has faith to enjoy liberty in what he eats is considered strong in faith. Those who are restricted by their conscience are plainly labeled as weak in faith. The Church has turned this around. Invariably, those who live with many restrictions are exonerated as strong in faith. Those who demonstrate freedom from endless restrictions are suspect of being weak in faith. Jesus, the founder of the Church, was comfortable in any setting. His first miracle was to make 300 gallons of wine for a wedding where the supply had been exhausted. If there were 600 guests, His miracle would potentially make one half of a gallon available for each of them. Later, He was criticized for frequenting the haunts of known sinners and accused of being an excessive drinker. Yet, He never sacrificed His liberty to reach the needy on the altar of conformance to self-righteous opinions.

This may be a helpful summarization: For those ensnared in legalism, all is forbidden, including that which is permitted. For those who have been set free in Christ, all is permitted, except that which is forbidden. For the unconverted, in their minds, all is permitted, including that which is forbidden.

Think about it.

Faith's Response

Lord, I ask that You give me revelation concerning these three questions: Do I express my viewpoints on non-essential issues in a manner which could thwart other's interest in embracing the absolutes of the faith? Am I succumbing to religious pressure in areas where You are offering me freedom? Would you assess me as a person who is laboring under religious legalism or as one whose life is enhanced because it is motivated by godly, spiritual values?

Chapter Twelve
PICKED, CLEANED AND PLACED

A Golf Tip

When conditions are extremely wet and muddy, even professional players are often given the pick, clean and place option. Without penalty, the ball can be picked up and cleaned. Then it can be placed at the nearest dry lie which is no closer to the hole. Scores are invariably lower when this gracious ruling is in effect.

The Word

Eph. 1:3-8 – Blessed be the God and Father of our Lord Jesus Christ, who has blessed us with every spiritual blessing in the heavenly places in Christ, just as He chose us in Him before the foundation of the world, that we should be holy and without blame before Him in love, having predestined us to adoption as sons by Jesus Christ to Himself, according to the good pleasure of His will, to the praise of the glory of His grace, by which He has made us accepted in the Beloved. In Him we have redemption through His blood, the forgiveness of sins, according to the riches of His grace which He made to abound toward us in all wisdom and prudence.

2 Tim. 1:9 – . . . who has saved us and called us with a holy calling, not according to our works, but according to His own purpose and grace which was given to us in Christ Jesus before time began.

Gleanings From the Word

You were picked by God before the foundation of the world to be adopted into His family. What an exhilarating thought! At some point in past eternity, your name and the plan for your life was on the agenda in the divine council of the Godhead. In the infinite wisdom of the Father, Son and Holy Spirit, who foreknew the good, the bad and the ugly about you, the Trinity perceived you as a prudent choice for the purposes of the Lord for your generation. You were handpicked by God because the very thought of all that you would become gave Him pleasure.

God predestined that, at a specific time, you would be confronted by the Holy Spirit with the revelation that Jesus is Lord. The moment you accepted the call, you were cleaned by the redeeming blood of Jesus. As your intermittent sins are confessed, you have perpetual forgiveness. At this very moment, you can come into the presence of God and bask blamelessly in His fatherly affection like a child who has no sense of guilt.

You have been placed in His Body with strategic gifts that were foreordained to be yours before time began. In the Greek, the phrase "made us accepted" in Ephesians 1:6 is the same as that which the angel Gabriel used to describe the Virgin when he called her "highly favored." Think of it. You are as distinctively gifted for what God has called you to do in your lifetime as Mary was for hers. No matter what you think about yourself—no matter what you think other people think of you—there is no one better suited to do what you have been called to do than you are. You have been privileged to be picked, cleaned and placed by God to sit by Him in heavenly places ruling over all the circumstances of life.

Faith's Response

Lord, I am so grateful that you picked me to be adopted into your majestic family. I thank you that I can come before You with no sense of blame. I know that I am cleaned and forgiven through faith in Your redeeming blood. This day help me to walk worthily of Your placement, utilizing the unique gifting with which You have graced me.

Chapter Thirteen

CUSSING AND CURSING

A Golf Story

If you have any "cuss" in you, golf will invariably expose it. In practically every round of golf, we are all challenged with the opportunity to explode with vulgar and profane expletives. To my regret, I have picked up that option on more than one frustrated occasion. Trust me: It does not help. Once, I angrily screamed out the Lord's name in an inappropriate manner after pulling a shot out of bounds. I was so intense about playing the next shot well that I could not be bothered with a quick prayer of contrition. Apparently, the Lord smiled and sighed, "Okay Jim, I will credit your most recent utterance of my Name as a sincere prayer request. And as you know, I am always faithful to answer prayer. If you want your game to go to perdition, I am more than happy to oblige you." For the rest of the round, I pulled nearly every shot. Seldom has my score been so high, nor my post-round repentance so earnest.

The Word

Prov. 18:21 – Death and life are in the power of the tongue, and those who love it will eat its fruit.
Prov. 26:2 – Like a flitting sparrow, like a flying swallow, so a curse without cause shall not alight.

Mk. 11:12-14,20-21 – Now the next day, when they had come out from Bethany, he was hungry. And seeing from afar a fig tree having leaves, he went to see if perhaps he would find something on it. When he came to it, he found nothing but leaves, for it was not the season for figs. In response Jesus said to it, "Let no one eat fruit from you ever again." And his disciples heard it. . . . Now in the morning, as they passed by, they saw the fig tree dried up from the roots. And Peter, remembering, said to him, "Rabbi, look! The fig tree which you cursed has withered away."

Rom. 12:14 – Bless those who persecute you; bless and do not curse.

Gleanings From the Word

There is a difference between cussing and cursing. In our idioms, "cussing" would entail the use of both vulgar and profane expletives. Though this is an unacceptable practice for those who desire to be conformed to the image of Christ, it is not one and the same as scriptural cursing. A curse is an oath sworn, either idly or sincerely, as a judgment on one's self or another over whom we have authority. The Word forbids this practice because the Lord has ordained that our words are to be agents of life and blessings rather than death and cursing.

Our speech shapes our lives and cultures. For instance, a parent may continually say to a child, "You are so stupid. You will never amount to anything." The child, when mature, finds it hard to make a living. To our shame, the vernacular for matriarchal incest has become a common expression in secular society. And incest is now cruelly rampant in our nation.

I have a very godly friend who is in the Lord's service. When she was a teenager, she became very distraught about the shape of her legs. When looking at them before a mirror, she would often say, "I hate my legs." Later in life, she developed severe leg problems for which the doctors could not fully account. When she sought the Lord in prayer, the Holy Spirit reminded her of the rash comments of her youth. He revealed to her that her words had been a curse against her legs that was being fulfilled. She instantly repented and renounced the statements she had made concerning her legs. Then she began to regularly praise God for healthy legs and bless them for their faithful service to her. Within days, her leg problems vanished, never to return.

Many of us need to follow suit in relation to what we have said about our own abilities and those of our children. Many adults' lives would be transformed if their parents would lovingly repent to them for the unkind remarks that were made to them in their youth. Any curse can be lifted as we prayerfully renounce it in Jesus' name and declare the opposite blessing of the Lord in its place.

Faith's Response

Lord, I bless You for the confidence You have placed in me by ordaining my words with power. Please forgive me for the rash things I have said concerning myself and others. In the name of Jesus and by the power of His blood, I now release myself and others from any curse which I might have uttered. Lord, I thank You that You have created me to be a blessing. I invite Your blessings to rest upon me and on all of those whose lives I might have unwittingly complicated through unwise speech.

Chapter Fourteen

THE WIND THAT IS A PERSON

A Golf Tip

On blustery days, wisdom dictates that you discern what the wind is doing before each shot and try to flow with it. If you are playing directly into a strong wind, never try to overpower it by swinging extra hard. Off the tee, tee it up lower and strike it with a smooth, relaxed swing. In the fairway, take a lower club and make your swing within your normal tempo. If you are approaching the green, consider making a knock down shot. This will keep the ball lower and diminish the potential for it to be stopped by the wind.

When the wind is behind you, let it work for you. Tee the ball up higher and consider using a three rather than a driver. This will cause the ball to fly further as it rides the wind.

The Word

Jn. 3:8 – The wind blows where it wishes, and you hear the sound of it, but cannot tell where it comes from and where it goes. So is everyone who is born of the Spirit.

Jn. 14:16-18,26 – And I will pray the Father, and He will give you another Helper, that He may abide with you forever the Spirit of truth, whom the world cannot receive, because it neither sees Him nor knows Him; but you know Him, for He dwells with you and will be in you. I will not leave you orphans; I will come to you. . . .

But the Helper, the Holy Spirit, whom the Father will send in My name, He will teach you all things, and bring to your remembrance all things that I said to you.

Jn. 16:7,13-15 – Nevertheless I tell you the truth. It is to your advantage that I go away; for if I do not go away, the Helper will not come to you; but if I depart, I will send Him to you. . . . However, when He, the Spirit of truth, has come, He will guide you into all truth; for He will not speak on His own authority, but whatever He hears He will speak; and He will tell you things to come. He will glorify Me, for He will take of what is Mine and declare it to you. All things that the Father has are Mine. Therefore I said that He will take of Mine and declare it to you .

Gleanings From the Word

The Scriptures use an analogy of the wind to illustrate the work of the Holy Spirit in the new birth, saying, "The wind blows where it wishes, and you hear the sound of it." However, the Holy Spirit is by no means an "it." He is a divine person who is a member of the Godhead. This marvelous person is worthy of our adoration. The Nicene Creed punctuates this beautifully as it states, "And I believe in the Holy Spirit, the Lord and giver of life, who proceedeth from the Father and the Son, and with the Father and the Son is worshipped and glorified, who spoke by the prophets."

Jesus emphasized the strategic importance of the Spirit as our helper in daily living. Though He was leaving His earthly ministry, He promised not to leave us as orphans to fend for ourselves. He said that He would send another in His place who would not be limited by time and space in His ministry to us. This helper, unlike Jesus prior to the resurrection, can give His undivided attention to everyone, everywhere, simultaneously. In one moment, He can give me direction in writing these lines, reveal Jesus to a lost sinner in Japan, and give you guidance concerning your marriage without experiencing one iota of stress.

The Holy Spirit is the administrator of all the treasured words and material blessings with which the Father and Son choose to bless us. He reminds us of the Lord's words and presents them as fresh life to our hearts. Through Him, we receive revelation concerning the spiritual and material blessings which the Lord has made available, and then He graces us with the faith to apprehend them.

When Jesus was on earth, He was the constant companion of His disciples. He walked with them, shared meals with them, provided for them, and inspired them. It is His intention that we each have the same caliber of companionship with the Holy Spirit as a person. If we are living with anything less, we are existing needlessly as spiritual orphans.

Faith's Response

Lord, I do not want to live as a spiritual orphan. Please forgive me for my inadvertent insensitivity to the person of your Holy Spirit. Holy Spirit, in Jesus' name, I now invite you to be my guide and companion. Please reveal to me all the wonderful things that have been freely given to me in Christ.

Chapter Fifteen
KNOCKED DOWN
A Golf Tip

A "knock down" shot is useful either when a heavy head wind is blowing or the limbs of a tree impede your approach. Choose a club that is two clubs stronger than the one you would normally use for the same distance; rather than a sand wedge use a nine. The ball should be a little further back in your stance with your hands in front of it at address. Keep your wrist and left arm stiff and take a three quarter back swing. On the down swing make a rapid transfer of weight to your left side. Hit crisply through the ball with a three quarter finish. This will keep the trajectory of the ball low and send it to the green.

The Word

Acts 9:3-6,8-9,17-20,26-27 – As he journeyed he came near Damascus, and suddenly a light shone around him from heaven. Then he fell to the ground, and heard a voice saying to him, "Saul, Saul, why are you persecuting Me?" And he said, "Who are You, Lord?" Then the Lord said, "I am Jesus, whom you are persecuting. It is hard for you to kick against the goads." So he, trembling and astonished, said, "Lord, what do You want me to do?" Then the Lord said to him, "Arise and go into the city, and you will be told what you must do." . . . Then Saul arose from the ground, and when his eyes were opened he saw no one. But they led him by the hand and brought him into Damascus. And he was three days without sight, and neither ate nor drank. And Ananias went his way and entered the house; and laying his hands on him he said, "Brother Saul, the Lord Jesus, who appeared to you on the road as you came, has sent me that you may receive your sight and be filled with the Holy Spirit." . . . Immediately there fell from his eyes something like scales, and he received his sight at once; and he arose and was baptized. So when he had received food, he was strengthened. Then Saul spent some days with the disciples at Damascus. Immediately he preached the Christ in the synagogues, that He is the Son of God. . . . And when Saul had come to Jerusalem, he tried to join the disciples; but they were all afraid of him, and did not believe that he was a disciple. But Barnabas took him and brought him to the apostles. And he declared to them how he had seen the Lord on the road, and that He had spoken to him, and how he had preached boldly at Damascus in the name of Jesus.

Gleanings From the Word

Perhaps one of the most strategic events for the benefit of the kingdom of God was the conversion of Saul (Paul). He had been cruelly aggressive in his zeal to purge Christians from the ranks of his fellow Jews. He was personally responsible for the imprisonment, torture and death of many Jewish men and women who had put their faith in Christ. As he was riding to Damascus, he literally "saw the light" and was "knocked down" with the revelation that Jesus was the Messiah.

The account of the Apostle Paul's response to his confrontation with the lordship of Jesus presents us with an excellent outline of what elements genuine conversion and discipleship are to contain. The moment Saul saw Jesus for the first time, he acknowledged Him as Lord. Then, without hesitation, he obeyed His words and went to Damascus to await further instructions. Through the ministry of Ananias, he was baptized in water and filled with the Holy Spirit. He then immediately began to fellowship with other believers. When Barnabas testified to the genuineness of Paul's salvation, he gave the Apostles the sure proof that Paul was truly a disciple. He explained to them that Paul had seen the Lord, that the Lord had spoken to him, and that Paul had boldly preached in the name of Jesus.

The pattern should be the same with you and me: We should remember a specific moment when we saw Jesus as our Savior and know that He spoke to us, bidding us to follow Him. This experience should be followed by instant obedience in what we feel He wants us to do. Subsequently, we should be baptized in water, filled with the Spirit, and join ourselves to a fellowship of believers. We are then to express the reality of the joy of our salvation by boldly telling others about Him.

Certainly the contemporary church would be more dynamic if this pattern were the expected norm for all new believers. We, unfortunately, seem to insist on complying with the Lord's commands on the installment plan. First we get saved. Then if we hear persuasive testimonies and sermons concerning the value of baptism in water and being filled with the Spirit, we eventually have those experiences. We fellowship with other Christians only as often as it can be fitted into our busy schedules. And of course, we will tell others about Christ if we have the assurance that it will not disturb their comfort levels.

Our Christian lives would be far more fulfilling if we would follow the Apostle Paul's example of zealous obedience. The simple requirement for one to be born-again is to repent of sin and confess Jesus as Lord. This gives us our permit for eternal life. However, to fully enjoy all the benefits of our salvation, we must obey all of His commands and follow through to apprehend all that He has for us.

Faith's Response

Lord, now I see that incomplete obedience is disobedience. I am willing to follow all of Your instructions. Please speak to my heart and tell me what I must do to make my obedience to You complete.

Chapter Sixteen
PASSPORT TO BETTER PUTTING
A Golf Tip

There is a passport to better putting that is available to every golfer who will take the time to change their thought picture while putting. Many putts are missed because the golfer uses too much wrist in their putts. This approach causes them to flick at the ball with the club head. The wrists have small muscles that are difficult to consistently control for speed, distance and direction. To change this course, golfers must adjust their thought picture in relation to what they want to move during putts.

Think of moving the shaft of the club, rather than simply the head. To facilitate this action, stand with your head directly over the putter head and ball. With a relatively loose grip, cock your wrist slightly ahead of the ball to the point where the face of the putter looks square, yet minutely slanted toward the ball. Take a smooth stroke in which the wrist remains cocked as you move the shaft straight back in your back swing and then straight forward toward the hole. On average-speed greens, you should make a back swing of around one and one-half inches for every 10 feet that your ball is from the hole. Your follow-through should be as long as your back swing. Do not allow your head to move until the ball has left your line of sight. Resist the temptation to guide the ball with the putter head. Let your ball speed and the contour of the green be the impetus to send the ball along your desired target line. If your putts have a tendency to go left, move the ball further back in your stance. If they tend to go right, move it further forward in your stance. On real close putts, it is helpful to move the ball a little further toward the tip of the club head, away from the normal sweet spot. When practicing at home, short carpet is a good representation of slow greens, and linoleum of faster greens.

The Word

Eph. 2:11-22 – Therefore remember that you, once Gentiles in the flesh—who are called Uncircumcision by what is called the Circumcision made in the flesh by hands that at that time you were without Christ, being aliens from the commonwealth of Israel and strangers from the covenants of promise, having no hope Give Honor and without God in the world. But now in Christ Jesus you who once were far off have been brought near by the blood of Christ. For He Himself is our peace, who has made both one, and has broken down the middle wall of separation, having abolished in His flesh the enmity, that is, the law of commandments contained in ordinances, so as to create in Himself one new man from the two, thus making peace, and that He might reconcile them both to God in one body through the cross, thereby putting to death the enmity. And He came and preached peace to you who were afar off and to those who were near. For through Him we both have access by one Spirit to the Father. Now, therefore, you are no longer strangers and foreigners, but fellow citizens with the saints and members of the household of God, having been built on the foundation of the apostles and prophets, Jesus Christ Himself being the chief corner stone, in whom the whole building, being joined together, grows into a holy temple in the Lord, in whom you also are being built together for a dwelling place of God in the Spirit.

Gleanings From the Word

God's Spirit has a revelation that He wants to impart to every Christian who desires passage into God's spiritual and material blessings. It is making the decision to cultivate a love for the nation of Israel and Jewish people everywhere. This is a secret passport which, for the most part, has been neglected by the Church throughout the centuries. Actually, though God in His mercy has blessed us, we have ignorantly refused this vital truth through our misdirected anti-Semitic thinking. Sadly, the subtle, and in some cases virulent, anti-Semitism that Christians have absorbed through the centuries has contributed greatly to the horrors of every Jewish persecution, including the Holocaust, and still is with us today. The Holy Spirit is now compelling us to repent.

We must come to understand that the Lord never intended that there be ongoing enmity between Christians and Jews. One of the primary reasons for Jesus' death on the cross was to break down the wall of enmity between us and reconcile us together to create one new man from the two. As we allow the Lord to cleanse anti-Semitism from our hearts, we qualify to mature and become the completed dwelling place of God in the Spirit. This is the clear teaching of the passage from the book of Ephesians in today's reading. Please note the words *two, both,* and *together.* They refer to the Gentiles who were afar off from, and the Jews who were near to, the covenants of God. It is through the blood of Jesus that we both have access through the Holy Spirit into the fullness of the Father's blessings. We are to be joined together as the habitation of God.

If we repent of our ignorant neglect of this vital truth, the Scriptures give ample precedents that the Father's blessings of prosperity, physical healing and household salvation will surely follow. Psalms 122:6-9 implies that as we love Israel and pray for her, prosperity will be our reward. When the Jewish elders of

Jesus' day wanted Him to come and heal a Gentile centurion's servant, they knew that they would have to give Him a good reason. When Jesus heard that the man loved the Jewish people and had built them a synagogue, He sent the Spirit of faith for healing to the man's home and healed the servant (Lk. 7:2-10). The first occurrence of the Holy Spirit being poured out on Gentiles to bring salvation and the baptism in the Holy Spirit to an entire neighborhood was prompted by the righteous acts of one Gentile man toward the Jewish people. The angel of the Lord clearly told Cornelius that his gifts to the Jews had come before God as a memorial of his kindness. As a result, God graced all of his friends and relatives with the gift of eternal life (Acts 10:1-5,24,34-48).

Faith's Response

Father, I ask forgiveness for any degree of prejudice and anti-Semitism that I have held in my heart. Lord, I thank You for all the blessings that You have afforded me through the contributions that Your chosen people have made to medicine, education and business. Lord Jesus, the Jews are Your kinsmen in the flesh, and I embrace them as my brothers in the Spirit.

Chapter Seventeen
FROM ROUGH STARTS TO TRIUMPHS
A Golf Tip

Like every golfer, I have those occasional days when I have an unusually rough start. When this occurs, it seems like I have forgotten how the game is played, and it causes me much grief. Somehow, the darker side of my temperament tends to process temporary ineptness in my game, as though it were an accurate barometer of my overall life and value as a person. If I allow this mindset to continue during the round, I often find myself brooding over every blunder that I have ever made. As ludicrous as it may seem, I foolishly perceive the results of a game as the indication that I have been permanently chained to a life of mediocrity.

Is there a way to change rough starts into triumphs? Yes! Here are three helpful steps:

1) Simply remind yourself that golf is a game and not a science. In golf, there is no formula that can guarantee identical results if the same constants are put into the equation each time you play. Certainly, there are a few nearly scientific aspects to the mechanics of a proper golf swing. But there are far more unpredictable challenges that are completely out of your control: unusually deep roughs, bunkers with sand of a consistency you are not accustomed to, and inconsistent greens from hole to hole. All of these are variables that make the game what it is. Any one of

these can cause scores to escalate. All it takes is one blade of grass to deflect a well hit putt. The most skilled putter would own up to the reality that there is an element of luck involved in a flawless day. Most professionals confess that most of their shots are imperfect as opposed to consistently perfect.

2) Write up instructions to yourself relating what you must do to make successful shots from drives all the way through to putts. When you perceive that you are in trouble, take it out and review it. Here is how mine reads on drives: Lay the club head flat on the ground with the sweet spot pointed toward the target line. Build your stance and grip—feet even and well under shoulders, and proper grip with the end of the left palm at least one inch below the end of the shaft. Keep your left eye behind the ball in a manner that makes the left shoulder feel as though it is also behind the ball. Take a slow smooth back swing, and follow through with a down swing that is only slightly faster.

3) Make a mental note of what you ate and drank during the 24-hour period prior to your rough start rounds. Many people have hidden problems with certain foods that can affect their coordination and sense of well being for as much as a day after they have ingested them. For me it is sugars and carbohydrates, because I am hypoglycemic. If I eat too much of either before playing, it can affect my score by ten or more strokes. I do best if I eat mainly protein before a round of golf.

If you will follow these three simple steps, it could be that you will find your rough starts graduating into triumphs. Then you can strut your stuff as you ascend to the 18th green with your regular foursome.

The Word

Rev. 12:9-11 – So the great dragon was cast out, that serpent of old, called the Devil and Satan, who deceives the whole world; he was cast to the earth, and his angels were cast out with him. Then I heard a loud voice saying in heaven, "Now salvation, and strength, and the kingdom of our God, and the power of His Christ have come, for the accuser of our brethren, who accused them before our God day and night, has been cast down. And they overcame him by the blood of the Lamb and by the word of their testimony, and they did not love their lives to the death."

Col. 2:13-15 – And you, being dead in your trespasses and the uncircumcision of your flesh, He has made alive together with Him, having forgiven you all trespasses, having wiped out the handwriting of requirements that was against us, which was contrary to us. And He has taken it out of the way, having nailed it to the cross. Having disarmed principalities and powers, He made a public spectacle of them, triumphing over them in it.

2 Cor. 2:14 – Now thanks be to God who always leads us in triumph in Christ, and through us diffuses the fragrance of His knowledge in every place.

Gleanings From the Word

Every child of God finds himself feeling as though he is inept spiritually, relationally or vocationally from time to time. When this occurs, the Bible is a tremendous source of encouragement, as it provides many marvelous faith concepts which can readily pull us back into a place of triumph. Today's reading offers a vivid example: No matter how we may feel about our circumstances, Christ has already granted us the victory, and we can choose to enjoy His triumph as our own. When He died on the cross and subsequently arose from the dead, He conquered every negative power that life can throw our way. He was victorious over Satan, sin, sickness and every real and imagined depressing, negative thought that could ever assault our minds. In the eternal realm, He defeated them and then humiliated them, as He dragged them in chains in a parade of triumph before all the host of heaven. The Christian faith dictates that all who put their trust in Jesus have a right to march with Him in a perpetual parade of triumph.

The term *triumph* is taken from the ancient Roman military world. It was a special parade which was granted to generals who returned to Rome after successful military campaigns. On an appointed day, the honored commander would be seated in a golden chariot drawn by exquisite white horses. His chariot would be followed by columns of the prisoners of war he had taken and various treasures that had been confiscated from the land he had conquered. All of Rome would line the streets to cheer him on and to view the evidence that revealed the magnitude of his victory.

This degree of honor certainly would be a confidence-boosting event for anyone privileged to experience it. However, the event was also designed with the opportunity for the victor to experience depression if he chose to do so. His personal valet, usually a slave who had accompanied him in his campaign would be seated on a black horse directly by his right ear. While the crowds were cheering him, this person—who knew him best—would berate him with insults: "Oh, they really see you as brave and honorable, but we really know the truth, don't we? It is true enough that your men bravely won the battle. But I saw you slinking back like a sniveling coward during the heat of that last skirmish. Tell me: Was it really necessary to burn that city and kill all those innocent women and children?" The general had a choice. He could enjoy the invigorating honor which had been bestowed upon him by the authorities over him. Or He could let the slave's reminders of his faults spoil what would have otherwise been a glorious occasion.

As Christians, when we put our faith in Christ, we were simultaneously invited to perpetually join Him in His triumphal chariot. Through our identification with Him, we were in Him when Christ met Satan and defeated him through His death and resurrection. As we triumphantly ride with Jesus, all the enemies of our lives are being dragged in chains behind us. However, we, too, have a slave who has positioned himself at our right ear. He comes in the form of our own inner voices, which condemn us as they rehearse our past sins and human flaws. Very often these voices are intensified in repetition and magnified in volume by the voice of the accuser, Satan. If we listen to them, the blessing of our triumph in Christ can be temporarily obscured. We can then begin to feel as though we have fallen out of the chariot and are being trampled under the feet of all of our enemies, whom Christ defeated on our behalf.

The choice is ours: We can listen to our inner voices of condemnation or enjoy the victory we have in Christ. Life is far more enjoyable and productive when we choose to envision ourselves as seated with Jesus in His triumphal chariot with all of our past inadequacies trailing in a spectacle of defeat behind us.

Faith's Response

Lord Jesus, I thank You because You have honored me by inviting me to join You in your triumph. Through faith, I now take my place beside You. Today is going to be both enjoyable and productive because of Your magnanimous grace toward me.

Chapter Eighteen

THE SACRED BOOK

A Golf Tip

The sacred book of golf is the United States Golf Association's rule book. In my experience, only a small percentage of golfers have even a nodding acquaintance with it. In almost every round, there are questions about the most elementary rules. In my opinion, every golfer who regularly plays owes it to himself or herself and his or her fellow players to be familiar with the game's rulings. Every golfer should own and read the rule book. For the sake of clarification, I will attempt to define a few of the most common and obscure rules and penalties.

Two Stroke Penalties

You must add two strokes to your actual number of strokes taken on the hole where you incurred the penalty. If you made three actual strokes, your total would be five. In the following instances, two stoke penalties are assessed.

1) If you hit the flagstick or its attendant while putting on the green.

2) If your ball is stopped or deflected by yourself or your partner's caddie, cart or equipment. There is no penalty if it strikes an opponent's person or equipment with a shot made before reaching the green.

3) Touching the ground, water, loose impediments, or boundary line of a hazard.

4) Playing the wrong ball, except in a hazard. Playing a ball that has been dropped or placed in the wrong place. This would include not replacing a marked ball back to its original position.

5) Improving your lie by moving the ball or altering any living obstruction to improve your swing or target line.

6) Repairing spike marks to improve you putting line. You may repair them without penalty if you have not yet made the green.

One Stroke Penalties

You must add one stroke to your actual number of strokes taken on the hole where you incurred the penalty. If you made four actual strokes, your total would be five. The following instances merit a one stroke penalty:

1) When the ball goes out of bounds or is lost in bounds, it will cost you stroke and distance. You must replay from the spot where the previous errant ball was originally struck.

2) When taking relief from a water hazard or an unplayable lie. If the ball went into the water, you may replay it from the spot of your previous stroke, or drop it two clubs length from an imaginary line of where it first crossed the hazard margin, but no closer to the hole.

3) Not telling your partners that you are about to lift a ball.

4) Cleaning a ball when not permitted. You may clean your ball only after it has settled on the green. If the ball is embedded in a hazard, you must play it as it lies or take a penalty for a drop. When your ball is embedded in the fairway, you may lift and clean it without penalty.

The Word

2 Tim. 3:16 – All Scripture is given by inspiration of God, and is profitable for doctrine, for reproof, for correction, for instruction in righteousness. . . .

1 Pet. 2:2 – As newborn babes, desire the pure milk of the word, that you may grow thereby.

Job 23:12 – I have not departed from the commandment of His lips; I have treasured the words of His mouth more than my necessary food.

Ps. 119:98 – You, through Your commandments, make me wiser than my enemies; for they are ever with me.

Ps. 138:2 – I will worship toward Your holy temple, and praise Your name for Your loving kindness and Your truth; for You have magnified Your word above all Your name.

Gleanings From the Word

What is the Bible? It is the inspired Word of God without error in its original manuscripts. It is God's Word, character and will expressed in written language. Any known language is limited, so it is essential that all who approach the Bible have a relationship with its Author, the Holy Spirit. Without the assistance of the Spirit, it can be a dry and perplexing book.

Psalm 119 is perhaps the greatest commentary on the Word of God contained in a single chapter of Scripture. This psalm makes reference to different aspects of the Word of God, such as His commandments, testimonies, precepts, statutes, judgments and His ways. The following is a descriptive list of these various types of readings within the Bible:

His *Law* is the entire Bible: our single most complete earthly resource for revelation concerning God's nature and His heart for man and all He has created.

Commandments make up the body of God's laws from which the Holy Spirit dictates specific obligations for righteous behavior to every individual in every generation and culture. His commandments are not necessarily the same for all nations. They can vary in their application and timing. For example, observing the Sabbath is an absolute for Jews under Moses, but a variable for contemporary Christians. Monogamous marriage relationships are an absolute in cultures where Christianity has been thoroughly established. However, this holy lifestyle can be destructive when presumptuously applied with immediateness to historically polygamous societies. Many children of second wives have been embittered against Christianity because unwise missionaries forced their fathers to divorce their mothers.

A *statute* is a ruling designed to accentuate the faithfulness of God's mercy or wrath. For example, God told Joshua that the curse of death would come upon the firstborn and last born of anyone attempting to rebuild ancient Jericho on its original site. He gave the sign of the rainbow after the flood of Noah's day as a sign that He would never again destroy the whole earth through flooding.

Precepts are distilled principles from God's Word that ensure successful living, such as love, wisdom, diligence and thrift.

Judgments are God's prescribed penalties or rewards for our behavior.

Testimonies are accounts of God's merciful actions on behalf of those who love Him.

The *Ways* of God are predictable responses to our circumstances as revealed by His nature as presented in the Bible. Abraham knew the ways of God, so he was able to remind God that it was not His way to destroy the righteous with the wicked when Abraham was told of His plans to destroy Sodom.

Here is a partial list of what God's Word will do for you:
- It will save your soul (Jms. 1:21).
- It will keep you from sin (Ps. 119:11).
- It will make you wise about your salvation (2 Tim 3:15).
- It will equip you for the good works to which the Lord has called you (2 Tim. 3:16-17).

- It will set you apart and show you the path to your inheritance among God's choice servants (Acts 20:32).
- It will give you a new heritage without the limitations of your genetic family line (Ps. 119:111; Prov. 3:8).
- It will heal your body (Prov. 4:21-23).
- It will give you encouragement and hope (Rom. 15:4).
- It will help you understand the benefits of affliction (Ps. 119:67,71,75).
- It will show you how to agree with God so your prayer life will be productive (Rom. 10:5-10).
- It will help you discern your motivations (Heb. 4:12).
- It will give you a successful life and guarantee that all you do will prosper (Josh 1:8).
- It will enable you to discern how to respond to contemporary issues. The Word of the Lord is right concerning all things (Ps. 119:128).
- It will encourage you to assist the poor on a temporary basis, but wisely discourage you from attempting to finance endless welfare for those who are under a curse for slothfulness and disobedience to God's laws (Lev. 19:10, Prov. 18:9).
- It will guide you in your choice of political candidates (1 Sam. 8).
- It will help you shape your attitudes toward the environment and the unborn (Lev. 19:9-14).

Your life will be transformed as you give yourself to the regular reading and memorization of His Word.

Faith's Response

Heavenly Father, I bless You for every copy of the Bible that is available to me. I plan to give it more of a priority in my daily schedule. As I do so, I ask that you anoint me with the Holy Spirit so I can fully benefit from what I read.

Chapter Nineteen
SAND SAVES
A Golf Tip

For most amateur golfers, the most dreaded of all hazards is a sand bunker. There are so many embarrassing stroke-costing mistakes that one can make, such as multiple attempts to get out and scalded shots that fly yards past the green. I have included some hints that may help you become more proficient in getting out of the sand nicely on the first shot. What could be sweeter than regularly being complemented for sand saves for par?

1) Your feet should be spread a little further apart than usual and your knees bent slightly lower than they would be for a fairway shot. Open your stance so your left foot is pointed 45 degrees to the left of your intended target line.

2) For shots of 20 yards or longer, grip your club toward the far end of the shaft. This adjustment will cause you to make a fuller swing. On shorter shots out of high lipped bunkers, you can choke down more on the shaft.

3) Your swing should be a firm but smooth motion that completes the letter "U" from your back swing, through your down swing and follow-through. Both the back swing and follow-through should end at the same height. Your downward motion should always be firm yet smooth. Keep your head down and still until you hear the ball hit on the green. You cannot afford to jerk your head in fear of flying sand. Moving your head will only increase your potential for a less than ideal shot.

4) For longer shots, close your club face to its natural lie as though you were going to hit a 60 yard shot off of the fairway. The closer the pin is and the higher the lip of the bunker, the more you will need to open your club face.

5) Many instructors emphasize hitting about two inches behind the ball. The idea is that your ball will come out on an exploding sand divot. This will work in unusually soft sand if you swing hard and follow all the way through with your U-swing. I have found that this method is not always reliable, particularly when hitting from wet or harder packed sand. In these instances, it is best to aim about 1/2 inch behind the ball. But remember to take a full U-swing and follow through completely.

6) Find a course that has a practice bunker and use it until you become confident. Most golfers would actually fair best if they warmed up with a sand wedge as opposed to a driver. Hitting out of sand loosens you up quicker. You do not have to pay for a bucket of balls, and it helps your game where you may need it most.

The Word

Ps. 2:8 – Ask of Me, and I will give You the nations for Your inheritance, and the ends of the earth for Your possession.
Ps. 74:20 – Have respect to the covenant; for the dark places of the earth are full of the haunts of cruelty.
Ps. 40:2 – He also brought me up out of a horrible pit, out of the miry clay, and set my feet upon a rock, and established my steps.
Prov. 11:30 – The fruit of the righteous is a tree of life, And he who wins souls is wise.

Gleanings From the Word

Very often, a Christian's friendship circles consist mainly of fellow believers. Since we primarily fellowship with Christians whose lives have been transformed by the power of the Holy Spirit, we can lose sight of the reality that there is a world full of people who do not know the Lord. Many may superficially appear as though they sincerely have harmonious lives. Yet each one of them has secret inner needs and an eternal necessity which can only be satisfied by a relationship with Jesus. Through the years, I have found that the golf links is a very fruitful mission field. It provides an opportunity for believers to break out of the confines of their limited friendship circles and meet new acquaintances of diverse backgrounds. The relaxed atmosphere of the 19th hole after a round of golf is an excellent forum to present Christ to those who might not yet know Him. The outline below, adapted from C.S. Lovett's *Witnessing Made Easy,* is a soul winning approach that is very effective for turning conversations toward spiritual matters. The beauty of it is that it is very simple to learn, and the format is designed in a way that flows smoothly from initial questions to an opportunity to present the Gospel. The only equipment that it requires is a pocket New Testament and a willing heart.

I.   *"Are you interested in spiritual things?"*
    A) Their response is irrelevant, as this question simply leads into the next one.

II. *"Have you ever thought about becoming a Christian?"*
    A) Here also, any response is a lead into the next question.

III. *"If a child were to ask you what a 'Christian' is, what would you tell them?"* If they give an answer which indicates that they know the Lord, ask them to share their testimony. If they can do so, you have made a new Christian friend; if not, you can continue.
    A) In response, most people will give you answers which actually describe how a Christian *might behave,* as

74

opposed to what a Christian *actually is*:

1) A Christian obeys the Ten Commandments.

2) Attends church regularly.

3) Is honest.

4) Does not drink, smoke or chew, nor go with girls who do.

B) Continue your inquiry with affirmations followed by the same question, *"Yes, that is true: most likely a Christian would attend church regularly and try to keep God's commands. But actually what is a Christian?"*

C) Continue this process until you sense that they understand inwardly that they really are not sure just exactly what a Christian is. Then you are to ask the following pivotal question:

IV. *"Would you allow me to take a few moments to show you from the Holy Bible just exactly what qualifies people to know that they are indeed Christians?"*

A) **Rom. 3:2** – For all have sinned and fall short of the glory of God.

1) After reading this, say, *"Let us examine this statement to see if it is true."*

   a) *"If Jesus were standing between us, would you say that either of us is as strategic to human history and as praiseworthy as He?"*

   1. Most will simply say "no," or just shake their heads to signal a "no."

   b) Gently ask, *"Why not?"* Any answer they give is simply a signal to lead into the next statement and question.

   c) *"We have all sinned at some time; for instance, we have all lied. How many lies would a person have to tell to be guilty of the sin of lying?"*

   Subtly lift your index finger up just below their

direct eye level. "One" is the answer which is
routinely offered. Then continue to the next verse.

B) **Rom. 6:23** – For the wages of sin is death, but the gift of
God is eternal life in Christ Jesus our Lord.

1) *"We both know that all of us have sinned and done
wrong things, and therefore, according to this verse,
we have a wage or a penalty coming for our sins,
which is eternal separation from God."*

2) *"However, there was an exchange made on the cross in
which God offers us a wonderful gift through Jesus.
He allowed Jesus Christ to pay the penalty for my sins
and your sins on the cross. He took all the punishment
due us that we might receive all the spiritual benefits
and blessings that were due to Him."*

3) *"This was God's gift to us, and through it, we have
eternal life in heaven with Him."*

4) Briefly explain to them that there is no way that a
person can actually earn a gift. It is given on the basis
of the grace of the giver rather than the behavior of the
recipient. Then proceed to the next verses.

C) **Jn. 1:11-12** – He came to His own, and His own did not
receive Him. But as many as received Him, to them He
gave the right to become children of God, to those who
believe in His name.

1) *"These verses reveal that the gift of eternal life and
becoming a Christian is one and the same as becoming
a child of God and a member of His family."*

2) *"Gifts are unique in that in order for a person to
receive one he must actually take personal possession
of it."*

3) *"If I told you that I was going to give you this Bible as
a gift, would you believe me? Do you have it yet?"*

4) Stretch forth your hand and offer the Bible to them,

asking them to pull it out of you hand. As it slips from your fingers, resist it a little, just so it will be imprinted in their mind that receiving a gift does take initiative.

5) Then explain to them that it could never actually be theirs until they took it from you hand and received it personally.

6) Continue by explaining that this is exactly how it is with the gift of eternal life that God is offering them; they must reach out and receive it personally. Then say, *"This is what this next verse is talking about."*

D) **Rev. 3:20** – "Behold, I stand at the door and knock. If anyone hears My voice and opens the door, I will come in to him and dine with him, and he with Me."

1) *"Here Jesus is saying that, if you will open the door of your heart, He will come in and stay with you forever."*

2) "If a good friend of yours was at your front screen door, and he knocked, and you could see that it was him, what would you say?"

a) Tap your finger on their sleeve or chest and say: *"Jesus is knocking on the door of your life right now. Would you like to invite Him into your life?"*

b) If they say "yes," lead them in a simple prayer in which they confess Jesus as Lord and the Son of God who was raised from the dead. Encourage them to ask forgiveness for their sins and invite Jesus to come and live in their hearts and take over their lives.

c) Once they have said the prayer, tell them that they have just received the gift of eternal life, which is the most precious of all gifts. Then ask them what they would say to a person who gave them a gift. Invite them to personally thank the Lord for the gift of eternal life.

d) Should they seem hesitant because they are shy, explain to them that they can pray at home or as they walk away to their cars. Pray for them, rehearsing for them the prayer that they might say. Ask the Lord to bless them as they pray later.

e) If they refuse, ask them this question: *"Do you understand that you are not rejecting me? Who is it that you are actually rejecting?"* Try to get them to say, "God." Then say, *"Are you sure that you really want to do that?"*

f) Close with a prayer in which they can hear you asking God to bless them and make them long for His presence and person.

Faith's Response

Father, the life You have given me through Christ is something that everyone needs. I ask You to direct me to a person today whose heart You have prepared to listen to the Gospel.

Chapter Twenty

MADNESS IN THEIR HEARTS

A Golf Tip

The game of golf has a mystifying propensity to expose the madness in our hearts. Without question, I see more displays of anger while golfing than I do in any other arena of life. Profane and vulgar expletives are screamed. Carts and golf bags are kicked. I have one friend who is prone to throw any club that misbehaves. (It frequently lands in trees.) He weighs well over 300 pounds, so watching him attempt to retrieve a club becomes rather entertaining. Personally, I am a ground pounder. Ashamedly, I confess, when my frustration breaks loose, I have been known to flail the ground with my club until a small ditch appears. Taking time to fill it in is always sobering and embarrassing.

It is not realistic to attempt to exempt oneself from the emotion of anger. It is an innate capacity of human personality. But we can all devise creative ways in which to monitor how it will be displayed. Here is what I do when I feel the madness begin to bubble in my soul:

1) I remind myself that it is just a game and that I have no right to spoil my fellow player's day.

2) I reason with myself that the source of my frustration is my pride. It indicates that, somehow, I think that I should be incapable of a missed hit. This notion is foolish, since even professional golfers make mistakes.

3) I express, sometimes loudly, "That was not my best effort." Then I follow it up with some remark of gratitude for the privilege of playing that day.

The Word

Ecc. 9:3 – This is an evil in all that is done under the sun: that one thing happens to all. Truly the hearts of the sons of men are full of evil; madness is in their hearts while they live, and after that they go to the dead.

Prov. 22:24 – Make no friendship with an angry man, and with a furious man do not go.

Mt. 5:22 – But I say to you that whoever is angry with his brother without a cause shall be in danger of the judgment. And whoever says to his brother, "Raca!" shall be in danger of the council. But whoever says, "You fool!" shall be in danger of hell fire.

Eph. 4:21-22,29-32 – If indeed you have heard Him and have been taught by Him, as the truth is in Jesus: that you put off, concerning your former conduct, the old man which grows corrupt according to the deceitful lusts. . . . Let no corrupt word proceed out of your mouth, but what is good for necessary edification, that it may impart grace to the hearers. And do not grieve the Holy Spirit of God, by whom you were sealed for the day of redemption. Let all bitterness, wrath, anger, clamor, and evil speaking be put away from you, with all malice. And be kind to one another, tenderhearted, forgiving one another, just as God in Christ forgave you.

Gleanings From the Word

My 82-year-old mother is a fine Christian lady, but she is also a pistol. At times, she allows herself the luxury of expressing her anger in very "down-to-earth" ways. Not too long ago, she rolled down her car window and initiated a fist-shaking, insult-yelling contest with a motorist who had cut her off. In shock, I began to laugh nervously and exclaimed, "Mom! you can't do that." She giggled and said, "Why not? He deserved it." My response was: "For openers, you are a Christian senior citizen, and you are to be a good example to those younger than you are. I am your little boy, and I also happen to be your pastor. So, would you please cool it?" We continued on our journey without further discussion of her misbehavior.

Anger is the feeling of sudden intense antagonism that arises from within us when we feel that our plans, pride or person is threatened. Exasperation is anger that brings on strong feelings of frustration because we do not know how or where to release it. Ephesians 4 acknowledges the reality that anger does exist. We all have the capacity for the emotion of anger, as it is a God-given gift to help us understand what we value. It is an indicator that alerts us as to whether or not we are valuing the right things or overvaluing the wrong things. When someone offends us or performs in a manner that jeopardizes an area for which we are responsible, it is legitimate to display controlled anger. It is possible to address the transgression without judging the worth of the guilty party as a person. No Christian has the option of wounding others with unrestrained displays of anger or letting a wound, which they have received, fester day after day.

This passage in Ephesians also identifies the most common ways in which inappropriate anger is exhibited. Here are some definitions for the words used for the various expressions of anger: *Corrupt words* are those uttered with the intention of hurting and discrediting another. *Bitterness* is repressed anger that seethes through one's personality and countenance. *Wrath* is anger that is accompanied by violent acts of reprisal. *Clamor* displays exasperation through boisterous arguing. And *evil speaking* is slanderous, foul-mouthed, abusive speech. None of these are options for those who want to imitate Christ.

So, how does one handle anger? Settle in your mind that you have no excuse to exhibit unrestrained outbursts of your emotions. Candidly speaking, no one is so short-fused that anger explodes out of them without their decision to let it do so. Anger can be felt as it begins to seethe within us. We have a choice as to how, when and where we will vent it. When you begin to sense your frustration rising, ask the Lord to help you examine why you are experiencing it. If it is the result of someone's inappropriate performance in relation to an important task, correct them and let them know that you are mildly displeased. Follow up by telling them why and how to improve their performance. If a loved one or friend has tread on your dignity or disrupted your plans, you can handle it the same way. However, once the offense has been stated, let it go. Relate to them in the same way you want God to relate to you. He looks forward to fellowshiping with us after we have been corrected and received His forgiveness. He does not remind us day after day of our past failures.

If you find that you are perpetually exploding over minor issues, most likely you are dealing with repressed anger. The Bible calls it "anger without cause." It causes us to manifest rage over minor incidents when actually we are angry about a much deeper issue. If this is the case, ask the Lord to help you identify the real reason that you are venting on the wrong things and people. It might be one of the following: Perhaps you have been unable to accomplish a goal that would be meaningful to your sense of self worth, or perhaps you have invested years in a relationship in which you have reaped rejection rather than appreciation. Whatever the case, take it to the Lord and ask Him to defuse the intensity of your rage and hurt. At times, it is good to vent your emotion in full voice to God. You will not scandalize Him, as He already knows how you feel. Afterward, from your heart, forgive those who have disappointed you.

Faith's Response

Lord, I am sorry for the poor way that I have represented You when I have given myself to unharnessed expressions of anger. I ask that You forgive me and give me the ability to control myself. I also ask You to heal all of those who have been wounded by my outbursts.

Chapter Twenty-one

THEY SPEAK IN TONGUES

A Golf Tip

When I first took up the game, I primarily played with seasoned players. Many of them made valuable contributions to my advancement in skill. However, they all neglected my education in one vital area: No one taught me the terminology used in golf. I call it "golfese." To me, it sounded like they were speaking in tongues. At times, my partners would rattle off expressions like the following: "Ah nuts! Your stance was too opened, and you sliced your ball O.B. That will cost you a stroke and distance penalty. If you want to draw the ball rather than slice it, you are going to have to remember to close your stance and pronate your grip. With that swing of yours, the best you can hope for is a fade. But don't worry about the Nassau, because we are in match and not medal play, and we are dormie."

At times, I wondered just when these fairway Pentecostals were going to ask me to handle snakes in order to improve my game.

I always encourage new players to purchase a book on the rules of golf, which has a glossary of the terms that are used in the game. Below are my definitions for the aforementioned terms. I assume the player is right-handed. A left-handed player would reverse the references to left and right.

• *Dormie* is an occasion in match play in which a player or team can not lose because they are ahead by the number of holes remaining in the round.

• A *draw* occurs when a ball's flight goes straight and then gently flows to the left before landing.

• A *fade* occurs when a ball's flight goes straight and then gently flows to the right before landing.

• A *gimme* is when an opponent concedes another player's next putt because it appears too close to the hole to miss.

• A *closed stance* is a stance in which the player's left toes rest on a line parallel to the target line with his right foot back from that line. This will generally cause a ball to move toward the left.

• *Match play* is a form of play in which the round is played hole by hole. The player or team with the lowest number of strokes on a hole wins that particular hole. Whoever wins the most holes wins the round.

• *Medal play* is a form of play in which the individual or team with the lowest total of accumulated strokes for 18 holes wins the round.

• A *Nassau* is a three-part bet in which a player can win or lose a pre-set amount of money on the front nine, the back nine, and the overall round. A five-dollar Nassau would mean that five dollars was wagered on each of the three respective parts. A player could win or lose no more than 15 dollars.

• *O.B.* indicates when a ball lands out of bounds. This costs the player a stroke and distance penalty. He must re-hit from the same spot and add two strokes to his accumulated total on that particular hole. One stroke is for his hit that flew out of bounds and the other is for the drop he had to take back to the spot from which his first shot was originally taken. For instance, if his tee shot went O.B., the next shot from the tee would be his third.

• An *open stance* is a stance in which the player's right toes rest on a line parallel to the target line with his left foot back from that line. This will generally cause a ball to move toward the right.

• To *pronate* is to grip the club with a gentle pressure in which each hand is pressed in toward the other. Pronating can assist in preventing slices, as it helps to keep the right elbow from moving too far outward on the back swing.

• A *slice* is when the ball takes an exaggerated curve from left to right.

• A *stroke* is any swing made with the purpose of hitting the ball.

The Word

Mk. 16:17-18 – "And these signs will follow those who believe: In My name they will cast out demons; they will speak with new tongues; they will take up serpents; and if they drink anything deadly, it will by no means hurt them; they will lay hands on the sick, and they will recover."

Rom. 8:26 – Likewise the Spirit also helps in our weaknesses. For we do not know what we should pray for as we ought, but the Spirit Himself makes intercession for us with groanings which cannot be uttered.

Jude 1:20 – But you, beloved, building yourselves up on your most holy faith, praying in the Holy Spirit. . . .

1 Cor. 14:2,13-19,23,28,39 – For he who speaks in a tongue does not speak to men but to God, for no one understands him; however, in the spirit he speaks mysteries. . . . Therefore let him who speaks in a tongue pray that he may interpret. For if I pray in a tongue, my spirit prays, but my understanding is unfruitful. What is the conclusion then? I will pray with the spirit, and I will also pray with the understanding. I will sing with the spirit, and I will also sing with the understanding. Otherwise, if you bless with the spirit, how will he who occupies the place of the uninformed say "Amen" at your giving of thanks, since he does not understand what you say? For you indeed give thanks well, but the other is not edified. I thank my

God I speak with tongues more than you all; yet in the church I would rather speak five words with my understanding, that I may teach others also, than ten thousand words in a tongue. . . . Therefore if the whole church comes together in one place, and all speak with tongues, and there come in those who are uninformed or unbelievers, will they not say that you are out of your mind? . . . But if there is no interpreter, let him keep silent in church, and let him speak to himself and to God. . . . Therefore, brethren, desire earnestly to prophesy, and do not forbid to speak with tongues.

Gleanings From the Word

I was raised in a fundamentalist Christian tradition in which our primary goal was doctrinal correctness. We dogmatically asserted that we were right about everything relating to faith and sound teaching. We were particularly intolerant and uncharitable in our attitudes toward anyone who endorsed the Pentecostal or charismatic practice of speaking in tongues. We basically dismissed them as unsophisticated, hyper-emotional people who would work themselves into religious frenzies and then begin to utter gibberish which they ignorantly labeled as biblical speaking in tongues. When questioned about the passage in the sixteenth chapter of Mark's Gospel, which indicates that speaking in tongues is a sign which can accompany those who believe in Christ, our response was often less than consistent. On one hand, if arguing the reality that the Bible is God's inerrant Word, we would proclaim that we believed every word in it from cover to cover, including the imprint which identified that our copy was bound in genuine leather. But when speaking in tongues was the issue, we would then condescendingly retort that Mark 16:9-20 was not found in the "most reliable" ancient manuscripts. We failed to mention that those same "reliable" manuscripts do not contain Genesis 1-46,

Psalms 105-137, Hebrew 9:14-13:25, nor the entire books of 1 and 2 Timothy, Titus, Philemon and Revelation.

There are three words which perfectly describe how I now feel about my former prejudice: "I was wrong!" The two factors that have convinced me of this truth are the plain teaching of God's Word and my own personal experience. One day in 1968, I was praying while driving down the interstate. I told the Lord that I wanted all that He had for me. Up to that point, I had never been exposed to hearing anyone speak or sing in tongues. Immediately after I uttered that prayer, I heard myself singing in a language that was completely foreign to me. I did not feel the least bit of emotion, nor any compulsion to continue, once I recognized that I was doing something unusual. I did not know that I had been sovereignly baptized in the Holy Spirit, or that I had been exercising the scriptural gift of unknown tongues. About six months later, I told a friend about my strange experience on the road to Memphis. He told me that I had received the infilling of the Holy Spirit with the accompanying evidence of speaking in unknown tongues. I was encouraged to incorporate the use of my prayer language in my daily devotions. Over the years, I have found prayer in tongues or praying in the spirit of great benefit.

Today's Scripture reading reveals a number of facts about the public and private use of tongues. When a person gives an utterance in an unknown tongue in a public context, it is essential that there be a subsequent interpretation. The interpretation of such an utterance is similar in function with the gift of prophecy. It can serve to edify and comfort those who hear it.

The Apostle Paul put a high premium on the value of praying in tongues privately. He stated that, when in public, he preferred to speak in a known language. Then he added that he spoke in tongues more than those who were guilty of the public abuse of the gift. The implications are that he frequently prayed and sang in the spirit or in an unknown language during his personal devotions.

Through praying in tongues, we can intercede about prayer needs that would normally be unutterable for us, simply because we are either not aware that they exist or need to be included on our prayer agenda. As we pray in tongues, we are speaking things to the Lord that are a mystery to us, but no mystery to Him, because He is the One who is orchestrating our prayers.

If you have never experienced this gift of tongues, I encourage you to explore the Scriptures and to interview believers who value it. If you follow the Holy Spirit's lead and begin to pray in the spirit, you can potentially experience several wonderful side benefits. You will find that you have a new sense of spiritual well-being or edification, because your measure of faith is being increased. There will also be occasions when you will sense that you are praising and giving thanks to God far more eloquently than the limits of your vocabulary.

Faith's Response

Lord, I apologize for my dogmatic position on spiritual matters in which I have only limited understanding and exposure. Your Word teaches that Your Holy Spirit will bring me into all truth. I ask You to lead me into Your truth in relation to prayer in unknown tongues. If I discover that it is valid to enhance my service to You, I pledge myself to seek it.

Chapter Twenty-two
DIVINE HEALING IS REASONABLE

A Golf Tip

If you want to enjoy golf with a minimum of time spent in recuperation, it is essential that you keep in mind that it is an athletic pursuit. Golf carries its own variety of sports injuries. Strained backs, blistered fingers, "golf elbow" and bruises from being hit by balls are all part of the package. Some common sense pointers for staying healthy follow:

1) Warm up by stretching properly before hitting any balls.

2) Always stay *behind* the person who is hitting. There is no such thing as a golfer who is so gifted that he cannot miss-hit a ball. On more than one occasion, I have been struck by the balls of good players who shanked their shots.

3) Use a glove and carry bandaids to cover blisters.

4) Keep your feet inside the cart, and do not drive too fast. I have been thrown from a cart when a reckless partner took a curve in the path too rapidly. It was painful for me and embarrassing for him.

5) Never try to swing yourself out of pain. If the hurting persists, simply quit. The game is not worth your health, and the fairways will be there on another day.

6) When lightning strikes, get off of the course immediately.

The counting method of one number for every mile is deceptive, because we naïvely presume that that distance is safe. I know of incidences where people have been killed by lightning bolts that originated more than 35 miles from their locations. Rain is uncomfortable, but you will recover quickly. Not so with lightning: you most likely will carry its consequences for life, or it will send you into eternity.

7) If you are allergic to insects bites or have a heart condition, keep your medication with you. Make sure to alert your partners about your condition and where you store your medication. Nitroglycerin tablets stored in the glove compartment of your car will not serve you if you have an emergency while on the golf course.

8) Above all, use sun block with at least a 30 SPF rating each time you play. Without question, the most common risk golfers share is that of developing skin cancer. No one is exempt from the possibility of this devastating killer. It is very sneaky in that it often takes 20 years or more to manifest after one's initial exposure to harmful ultraviolet rays. If you have fair skin and are well marked with freckles and moles, you need to consider adding a broad-rimmed hat, long-sleeved shirts and slacks to your sun protection weaponry.

The Word

Ps. 121:6 – The sun shall not strike you by day, nor the moon by night.
Ps. 107:16-20 – For He has broken the gates of bronze, and cut the bars of iron in two. Fools, because of their transgression, and because of their iniquities, were afflicted. Their soul abhorred all manner of food, and they drew near to the gates of death. Then they cried out to the LORD in their trouble, and He saved them out of their distresses. He sent His word and healed them, and delivered them from their destructions.

Ps. 103:1-3 – Bless the LORD, O my soul; and all that is within me, bless His holy name! Bless the LORD, O my soul, and forget not all His benefits: who forgives all your iniquities, who heals all your diseases.

Ex. 15:26 – "If you diligently heed the voice of the LORD your God and do what is right in His sight, give ear to His command-ments and keep all His statutes, I will put none of the diseases on you which I have brought on the Egyptians. For I am the LORD who heals you."

James 5:14-16 – Is anyone among you sick? Let him call for the elders of the church, and let them pray over him, anointing him with oil in the name of the Lord. And the prayer of faith will save the sick, and the Lord will raise him up. And if he has committed sins, he will be forgiven. Confess your trespasses to one another, and pray for one another, that you may be healed. The effective, fervent prayer of a righteous man avails much.

Gleanings From the Word

The Bible presents us with a loving heavenly Father who is in-terested in every aspect of our lives. Our physical health and finan-cial solvency is important to Him. He is concerned about our physical welfare, because our bodies were created to glorify Him and to reflect His loving character. The wonderful thing is that He does not abandon us even when our afflictions are due to our own foolish negligence. When we call upon Him, He is faithful to an-swer us and to heal us from all of our sicknesses.

If we want to position ourselves to receive divine healing, it behooves us to become thoroughly convinced that it is reasonable to expect it from our Father God who loves His children.

Jesus and all the apostles preached repentance as they pro-claimed the Good News of the Gospel. John the Baptist told the Pharisees that his ministry of preaching repentance was like an ax cutting through the root of a tree (Mt. 3:8-10). When we repent and turn to God, it severs Satan's legal hold on us. Because of Adam's fall, we were all lost to Satan, sin and sickness. The end result of the fall was spiritual and physical death. The most common way in which mortal death is accomplished is through sickness. Sin and rebellion against God are the primary roots of the tree of man's fallen condition. Sicknesses and pain are like that tree's limbs and branches. Death is the fruit that they will eventually produce. As we are born-again and receive Jesus as our Savior and Lord, He cleanses and forgives us of all of our transgressions. Through salvation, the Lord puts the ax to the root of our condition and makes us into a new creation. At this point, the root of our former fallen condition is legally severed by the power of God's ax. Its accompanying branches of sickness and the fruit of untimely death no longer have a legal right to rule in our lives.

Whenever Christians call upon the Lord to forgive them of recent sins, there is also power available to heal them of their sicknesses. The same power that forgives sins heals diseases. This is the clear teaching of James 5:14-16.

When a person who is sick calls for others to pray for his physical healing, there is simultaneous power to both heal the sickness and to forgive any sins that he might have committed. When a person who is sick confesses his sins, physical healing is apt to follow if he understands that the power for it is available.

It is reasonable to believe God is willing to heal sicknesses because He is most definitely interested in our physical bodies. After all, we were made in His image and were created to reflect His glory. He certainly did not design us in a sick condition. To the contrary, He programmed the human body to automatically attempt to heal itself whenever sickness strikes. Therefore, it is not unreasonable to expect Him to be more than willing to add an extra boost of grace when we ask Him to speed up the healing process, which our bodies are already attempting. Very simply, you can serve Him more effectively and longer by being healthy than you can by being sick.

Faith's Response

Lord, I present my body to You for health and a long, fruitful life. I thank You for your willingness to answer my prayers for healing when sickness does afflict me. I am grateful for modern medicine, but you are my first recourse. I will do all I can to honor this wonderful temple which you have given me. From this point on, I will look to You to enhance and accelerate the healing propensity that You have so graciously placed within my body.

Chapter Twenty-three
VILIFIED TODAY, VINDICATED TOMORROW

A Golf Tip

Frequently, I encounter die-hard purests who vilify most every advancement that modern technology has brought to golf equipment. Their claim is that success rests solely upon the correct swing technique. My experience with run-of-the-mill amateur golfers has disproved their theory in many instances.

I have a very good friend whose name is Fred Adinolfi. He has golfed for over 30 years and has above-average ability. He is a serious student of the instructional material that is readily available from master teachers. His problem was that he had outdated equipment that did not allow him the opportunity of surviving hits that were less than perfect. I encouraged him to use my "Big Bertha" metal woods and irons. My belief was quickly vindicated. His game improved drastically in distance and accuracy. He was so impressed that he has recently updated all of his clubs.

If your clubs are antiquated and your game is stagnant, I heartily implore you to get new equipment. If money is a factor, good brand name clubs are always available at reduced prices from folks like myself. I am the manufacturer's dream: If it's new, I want to try it. In the past 12 years, I have bought ten sets of irons and countless woods. To date, I have not regretted one purchase.

However, I will admit that if every purchase would perform as advertised, my handicap would be a minus 30.

The Word

Hab. 1:5 – Look among the nations and watch. Be utterly astounded! For I will work a work in your days Which you would not believe, though it were told you.

Ps. 98:1 – Oh, sing to the LORD a new song! For He has done marvelous things; His right hand and His holy arm have gained Him the victory.

Heb. 8:6-13 – But now He has obtained a more excellent ministry, inasmuch as He is also Mediator of a better covenant, which was established on better promises. For if that first covenant had been faultless, then no place would have been sought for a second. Because finding fault with them, He says: "Behold, the days are coming, says the LORD, when I will make a new covenant with the house of Israel and with the house of Judah, not according to the covenant that I made with their fathers in the day when I took them by the hand to lead them out of the land of Egypt; because they did not continue in My covenant, and I disregarded them, says the LORD. For this is the covenant that I will make with the house of Israel after those days, says the LORD: I will put My laws in their mind and write them on their hearts; and I will be their God, and they shall be My people. None of them shall teach his neighbor, and none his brother, saying, 'Know the LORD,' for all shall know Me, from the least of them to the greatest of them. For I will be merciful to their unrighteousness, and their sins and their lawless deeds I will remember no more." In that He says, "A new covenant," He has made the first obsolete. Now what is becoming obsolete and growing old is ready to vanish away.

Gleanings From the Word

Church history has been described as 2,000 years of men attempting to build the kingdom of God without the presence and power of the Holy Spirit. Invariably, religious leaders initially resist every blessed gift and useful tool that the Holy Spirit attempts to share with the Church. However, the Holy Spirit always wins in these struggles—whatever we are vilifying today, He vindicates tomorrow. The following is a list of practices that we treasure today that were originally reviled by our ancestors in the faith:

- The Bible in the language of the common man
- The singing of congregational hymns
- Baptism in water by immersion
- The understanding that it possible to have the assurance that one is saved and is going to heaven
- The policy that congregations have the right to insist that their pastors have a personal born-again experience
- Evangelizing African-Americans
- Foreign missions
- Open air preaching
- Spontaneous extemporaneous preaching (Historically, pastors read their sermons.)
- Altar calls
- Sunday School
- Laymen preaching
- Home prayer meetings
- Church buildings being filled day and night weekly (Proper churches of the past would have services only on the Sabbath or on specified days during "decent hours.")
- Prayer for the healing of the sick
- Radio and television

Most contemporary Christians who read this list are shocked that these things could have been resisted by their spiritual ancestors. But the fact is that they were, tooth-and-nail. The most obvious reason is our forefathers could find no precedent for such practices within their own biblical understanding nor traditions. They later discovered that these practices had either explicit or implied foundations in Scripture. Perhaps one of the major hidden reasons we resist things that appear or sound revolutionary or strange is because they do not fall within our preference or comfort zones. A person who prefers traditional hymns might be uncomfortable in a service where Scripture choruses are sung. Those who have never lifted their hands feel like those who do so are fanatical showoffs. In both cases, the offended parties might be very apt to dogmatically comment that they were sure that the services where these things occurred were a grievance to the Holy Spirit. Religious people frequently interpret their subjective feelings as the viewpoint of the Almighty.

Surely church life and religious relationships would flow more harmoniously if we all realized that our discomfort when our personal preferences have been offended is not synonymous with the Holy Spirit being offended. The fact is, when it is God's desire to position His Church for greater blessings and fruitfulness, He has never obligated Himself to operate within anyone's comfort zones. It is not beyond Him to offend our minds in order to bless our hearts.

Faith's Response

Lord, I do not want to resist Your move in the earth or within Your Church. I hereby ask You to give me the grace to be open to explore the new spiritual insights without regard for my own traditional comfort zones. It is my intention to embrace every good gift that You introduce to better prepare me to fulfill my destiny in Your glorious army.

Chapter Twenty-four

THE IMPORTANCE OF DECISION

A Golf Tip

Anyone who regularly plays the game of golf soon learns the importance of decision. Consistent success is dependent upon two primary elements: skill and the ability to make strategic decisions relating to each shot's club selection and target line. Observation has persuaded me that a golfer who is a thinker will usually defeat one of greater skill who is not.

You might want to consider the following shot decisions in certain scenarios:

• You are in a low-lipped sand trap with packed sand or on hard, thin grass 20 yards from the green. When in doubt, putt it. I have made many pars using my putter when I was unsure of my ability to get another club under the ball successfully. A mediocre putt is often better than a good wedge in some situations.

• Your ball is surrounded by obstructions. Always take the shortest and clearest way out. A short shot that positions you with a good second opportunity is superior to a chancy longer shot that may put you in further jeopardy.

• The ball lies on a downhill slope with 150 yards of water to cross. The temptation is to attempt one of those invigorating miracle shots with a fairway wood. The problem is, miracles are rare. Use a higher lofted club that you are confident can carry the water. To avoid hitting it fat and pulling it left, choke down and set up with a target line to the right of your intended landing spot.

• A tight pin is protected by water and front side bunkers. Choose a stronger club. A long putt or the need for a chip from behind the green is far less costly than a water penalty or a sand shot.

The Word

Mt. 25:19-29 – After a long time the lord of those servants came and settled accounts with them. So he who had received five talents came and brought five other talents, saying, "Lord, you delivered to me five talents; look, I have gained five more talents besides them." His lord said to him, "Well done, good and faithful servant; you were faithful over a few things, I will make you ruler over many things. Enter into the joy of your lord." He also who had received two talents came and said, "Lord, you delivered to me two talents; look, I have gained two more talents besides them." His lord said to him, "Well done, good and faithful servant; you have been faithful over a few things, I will make you ruler over many things. Enter into the joy of your lord." Then he who had received the one talent came and said, "Lord, I knew you to be a hard man, reaping where you have not sown, and gathering where you have not scattered seed. And I was afraid, and went and hid your talent in the ground. Look, there you have what is yours." But his lord answered and said to him, "You wicked and lazy servant, you knew that I reap where I have not sown, and gather where I have not scattered seed. So you ought to have deposited my money with the bankers, and at my coming I would have received back my own with interest. Therefore take the talent from him, and give it to him who has ten talents." For to everyone who has, more will be given, and he will have abundance; but from him who does not have, even what he has will be taken away.

Joel 3:14 – Multitudes, multitudes in the valley of decision! For the day of the LORD is near in the valley of decision.

Jos. 24:15 – And if it seems evil to you to serve the LORD, choose for yourselves this day whom you will serve, whether the gods which your fathers served that were on the other side of the River, or the gods of the Amorites, in whose land you dwell. But as for me and my house, we will serve the LORD.

1 Kings 18:2 – And Elijah came to all the people, and said, "How long will you falter between two opinions? If the LORD is God, follow Him; but if Baal, follow him." But the people answered him not a word.

Ps. 115:15-16 – May you be blessed by the LORD, who made heaven and earth. The heaven, even the heavens, are the LORD's; but the earth He has given to the children of men.

Deut. 30:19 – I call heaven and earth as witnesses today against you, that I have set before you life and death, blessing and cursing; therefore choose life, that both you and your descendants may live.

Gleanings From the Word

In 1968, I heard one of the most revolutionary sermons that I had ever heard prior to that occasion. It was entitled, "The Importance of Decision." The minister used the passages given in today's reading as his proof text. The following paragraph is an abbreviation of the riveting insights he expounded for the next hour:

God has entrusted man with the capacity to make a faith decision as to what kind of life he will have. You must choose between prosperity or poverty, success or failure, health or infirmities, a harmonious, tranquil family life or a tension-filled home, death or life, a life filled with blessings, or one checkered with the curse of a disproportionate number of hardships. God has delegated the choice to you. You must make a firm decision as to what you want. If you trust Him, He has obligated Himself to underwrite your decision. But it is essential that you settle the issue in your heart and mind through faith in God's reliability. Then you must steadfastly refuse to accept any permanent alternatives.

When that minister gave the invitation, I rushed to the altar and followed him in a prayer similar to the one in the Faith's Response at the end of this section. As I said the prayer, something clicked in my heart. Without hesitation, I can boldly state that God has been faithful. I have led an enjoyable, prosperous, successful life in the midst of occasional adversities that have crumpled men far more gifted than me. In many ways, the stage was set for me to lead a life filled with excuses for dysfunctional performance at home and vocationally. My father had been in the military, and we had been transferred 14 times between my first and ninth year of school. I never took school or any preparation for life seriously. I was a 220-pound party animal who had been fortunate in landing a good job as a manufacturer's representative with a major apparel firm. My boss did not perceive me as a strategic player, so he assigned the territory with the least apparent potential for productivity to me. Six months after saying that prayer, I had lost 60 pounds and was the number one producer in my division. I was asked to give motivational lectures for the sales force of the entire company. Several years later, my department was phased out, and the other salesmen were fired. I was promoted to a better division, in a smaller territory with at least a 30 percent increase in commissions.

Each one of us has three pivotal decisions to make about our lives: who we will worship, who we will marry, and what is to be our life's vocation. In addition, we each are called upon to make other decisions that are also clearly strategic. One very important decision is not to be intimidated by our own assessment of our individual gifting limitations. We are not all created equal with regard to our natural talents. A few multiply gifted people seem to lead charmed lives of unbroken success. However, far more people are leading lives that decry the potential that others observe in their abilities. Most of us are like the man in Matthew 25: We just have one talent. However, a single talent in present day currency would be valued at over one million dollars. Therefore, being limited to only one talent can hardly be seen as limiting our opportunities. Our one talent can be perceived as a golden opportunity which, through faith and diligence, has the potential to grow into a sizable fortune. Faith in God puts those of us with minimal talents on an even playing field with those who appear multiply gifted. If we trust God, He will increase our productivity to the extent that our blessings far exceed those whose talents are not coupled with faith.

Faith's Response

Father, this day You have put a very important decision before me: I can choose life or death, blessing or cursing. I therefore choose life and blessings. Through faith in You, I will live a healthy, successful and prosperous life—physically, vocationally and relationally. I thank You for entrusting me with a choice.

Chapter Twenty-five
WHOLE IN ONE
A Golf Story

On June 20th, 1995, I was involved in an auto accident that robbed me of 70% of my sight. I was traveling no more than 25 mph, and the airbag should not have deployed. It scraped layers of tissue from my eyeballs. My head struck the sharp edges of the steering wheel housing and cut into both eyes. The pupil and cornea of my left eye were caved in to the point that they were inverted. The retinas of both eyes were severely compromised. One-third of my right eye's iris was ripped away. Both eyeballs became swollen to the size of golf balls and were protruding from the sockets. I was rendered legally blind. In the emergency room, my first words to the eye specialist were, "When will I be able to read my Bible and golf again?"

Three months later, I leaped for joy when the doctor reluctantly gave me permission to golf. I could hardly see my own fingers at arms length. The ball was a blur, and my partner had to point me toward the green. The good news about the blindness was that it forced me to keep my head down and my swing slow and smooth. That first round, I shot an 87. Two weeks later, God gave me a hole in one on a 170 yard par 3. My partners that day happened to be Jewish. They all agreed that converting to Christianity might be a wise move for their golf handicaps!

The Word

Acts 4:10 – Let it be known to you all, and to all the people of Israel, that by the name of Jesus Christ of Nazareth, whom you crucified, whom God raised from the dead, by Him this man stands here before you whole.

1 Thes. 5:23 – Now may the God of peace Himself sanctify you completely; and may your whole spirit, soul, and body be preserved blameless at the coming of our Lord Jesus Christ.

2 Cor. 12:9 – And He said to me, "My grace is sufficient for you, for My strength is made perfect in weakness." Therefore most gladly I will rather boast in my infirmities, that the power of Christ may rest upon me.

Rom. 8:28 – And we know that all things work together for good to those who love God, to those who are the called according to His purpose.

Gleanings From the Word

There is no hardship that Satan or life can throw your way that can undermine the reality of your wholeness in Christ. His joy is to present you to the world as "whole in One"—whole in one Lord, one body, mind and spirit—in the depths of every challenge that you face. I think that perhaps He permits us to appear weak, so people will be attracted to faith in Him as they witness the strength that He gives us.

During my college years, there were few Christians whom I found impressive. "Bopping" Bob was the exception. He was born with a spastic condition which caused his whole body to twitch convulsively every time he attempted to move. Spittle incessantly dripped from his lips when he spoke. Nonetheless, his faith was dynamic, and he knew that nothing could prevent him from having a successful life.

Early in his college career, he married a girl with a similar condition. God gave them a beautiful, healthy baby. Bob earned an excellent living for his family. He worked his way through school as a door-to-door salesman for a publisher of personalized holiday cards. To write up an order, he would place the form on the floor and hold it in place with his knees. He would then steady his writing hand with his free hand and write the order. All who encountered him were taken back by his appearance of overwhelming helplessness. But within moments, they would recognize that he perceived himself as perfectly normal. Surely, the inner voice of God spoke to all who observed him and questioned, "Are you really as whole as he?"

Call upon the name of Jesus, and He will present you as whole—spirit, soul and body. There is no other name given among men that can enable you to function as whole in the midst of weakness.

Faith's Response

Father, forgive me for using my obvious weaknesses as an excuse to exempt myself from diligent efforts to achieve great things for Your honor. Today, with your help, I will walk as whole in One. I will not be paralyzed by the fear of exposure. I am confident that in spite of my flaws, Your gift of strength will be demonstrated through me.

Chapter Twenty-six

FASTING

A Golf Story

After being blinded in that car accident, I was forced to take a three month sabbatical from golf. The doctor's prognosis was that I would be legally blind for the rest of my life. They attempted to discourage me from the hope of playing again due to the fragile condition of my eyes. I would not be thwarted. I bought a set of "Big Bertha" graphite irons as a token of my determination to resume playing.

My layoff was more difficult for me than fasting from both food and water. But as I shared in the previous chapter, I shot a round of 87 on my first trip back to my par 72 home course. It was unbelievable: I was using new clubs, and I could not distinguish familiar faces at a distance of more than 10 feet. I concluded that my involuntary golf fast had actually been helpful. Since that time, I have put myself on a one-week fast whenever my game falls into a slump. It is never easy, but always rewarding.

The Word

2 Chr. 7:14 – If My people who are called by My name will humble themselves, and pray and seek My face, and turn from their wicked ways, then I will hear from heaven, and will forgive their sin and heal their land.

Mt. 6:16-17 – "Moreover, when you fast, do not be like the hypocrites, with a sad countenance. For they disfigure their faces that they may appear to men to be fasting. Assuredly, I say to you, they have their reward. But you, when you fast, anoint your head and wash your face. . . ."

Joel 2:15-19 – Blow the trumpet in Zion, consecrate a fast, call a sacred assembly; gather the people, sanctify the congregation, assemble the elders, gather the children and nursing babes; let the bridegroom go out from his chamber, and the bride from her dressing room. Let the priests, who minister to the LORD, weep between the porch and the altar; let them say, "Spare Your people, O LORD, and do not give Your heritage to reproach, that the nations should rule over them. Why should they say among the peoples, 'Where is their God?'" Then the LORD will be zealous for His land, and pity His people. The LORD will answer and say to His people, "Behold, I will send you grain and new wine and oil, and you will be satisfied by them."

Isa. 58:6-12 – "Is this not the fast that I have chosen: to loose the bonds of wickedness, to undo the heavy burdens, to let the oppressed go free, and that you break every yoke? Is it not to share your bread with the hungry, and that you bring to your house the poor who are cast out; when you see the naked, that you cover him, and not hide yourself from your own flesh? Then your light shall break forth like the morning, your healing shall spring forth speedily, and your righteousness shall go before you; the glory of the LORD shall be your rear guard. Then you shall call, and the LORD will answer; you shall cry, and He will say, 'Here I am.'" If you take away the yoke from your midst, the pointing of the finger, and speaking wickedness, if you extend your soul to the hungry and satisfy the afflicted soul, then your light shall dawn in the darkness, and your darkness shall be as the noonday. The LORD will guide you continually, and satisfy your soul in drought, and strengthen your bones; you shall be like a watered garden, and like a spring of water, whose waters do not fail. Those from among you shall build the old waste places; you shall raise up the foundations of many generations; and you shall be called the repairer of the breach, the restorer of streets to dwell in.

Gleanings From the Word

Fasting is abstaining from food for spiritual purposes. The degree and length of one's fast can vary, depending upon health and conviction. While fasting, many take only liquids, such as water and juices. Others intermittently fast from certain meals or types of food on selected days. A total fast from both food and water should never last more than three days and should not be considered without consulting a physician. Anyone with a history of health problems should get medical advice before embarking on any type of fast.

Fasting is a neglected Christian discipline that can be very rewarding for those who will practice it. I call it a discipline because Jesus gave instructions on prayer, giving and fasting. It appears that He expects His disciples to practice all three. He did not say, "If you fast." He said, "When you fast."

There are numerous biblical purposes for fasting. It often is the key to break the yoke of stubborn health, marital and financial difficulties. When the believers of a troubled nation enter corporate periods of fasting, it often brings healing to their land. Corporate fasting can be a forerunner to a nation's spiritual and economic revival. The following poem from Arthur Wallis' book, *God's Chosen Fast,* gives ample scriptural precedents for this Christian discipline:

They Fasted

On Sinai's Mt., with radiant face. To intercede for heaven's grace. Upon a stubborn wayward race. He fasted.

Once lifted from the miry clay. When opposition came his way. This soldier king would often pray with fasting.

A seer, possessed of vision keen, who told the troubled king his dream. Had light on God's prophetic scheme through fasting.

This prophetess in temple court beheld the Babe the tow had brought; For Him she long had prayed and sought while fasting.

He came to break the yoke of sin. But, ere His mission could begin He met the foe and conquered him while fasting.

"Set these apart," the Spirit bade. A spring, that soon vast rivers made, Broke open by men who as they prayed were fasting.

So shall they fast when I am gone; Was this no word to act upon? Ask countless saints who fought and won with fasting.

When we shall stand on that great day and give an account, what shall we say, if He should ask us "Did you pray—with fasting?"

Faith's Response

Lord Jesus, I am Your servant, and I want to flow in obedience to Your commands. There are circumstances in my life that have not yet responded to the level of blessings that are set forth in the Word. I ask You to intervene as I give myself to a period of fasting accompanied by prayer.

Chapter Twenty-seven
SOWING AND REAPING

A Golf Tip

When I was in my teens, I saw a movie entitled, "Harvey," which featured Jimmy Stewart in the starring role. His character was that of a friendly chap who kept company with an invisible giant rabbit whom he called Harvey. He constantly carried on conversations with the rabbit and cordially introduced him to everyone he met. As a result, his family attempted to have him institutionalized. In one scene, Jimmy Stewart spoke a line that I have incorporated into my philosophy of life. His therapist asked him why he did not angrily retaliate toward those who were mistreating him. He drawled in reply, "A long time ago, I began to understand that I could be either clever or pleasant, and I chose to be pleasant." I have found that, as I have sown pleasantness into others, I have invariably reaped it everywhere I go.

On the golf course, I have found that the principles of sowing and reaping are most rewarding. Before my accident, I chose to always present a pleasant demeanor to everyone I met. No matter where I played, it was my habit to exhibit friendliness toward members of the course staff. When playing with senior citizens, I retrieved their water balls, raked their traps, and helped them locate lost balls. During the two years that I was legally blind, I reaped a gracious harvest. Each morning, my wife would drop me off at one of the local courses. Weather permitting, I would play two rounds, and she would pick me up in the evening. I could not drive a cart, so I would be joined with others who at times were complete strangers. Without exception, they treated me with even more kindness than I had previously sown in others. They helped me get the right club from the bag for each shot and assisted in my lineup for each shot. Considerate fellow players raked my traps and retrieved my lost and water balls. On the occasions when my wife could not give me a ride home, I was chauffeured by gracious new golfing friends.

Golf is a genteel sport. It is meant to be played in an atmosphere of courteous etiquette and friendly competition. If you sow genteel behavior by complying with the game's protocols of etiquette, you will likely reap years of pleasant rounds.

The Word

3 Jn. 1:2 – Beloved, I pray that you may prosper in all things and be in health, just as your soul prospers.
2 Cor. 9:6 – But this I say: He who sows sparingly will also reap sparingly, and he who sows bountifully will also reap bountifully.
Lk. 6:38 – "Give, and it will be given to you: good measure, pressed down, shaken together, and running over will be put into your bosom. For with the same measure that you use, it will be measured back to you."
Prov. 3:9-10 – Honor the LORD with your possessions, and with the firstfruits of all your increase; so your barns will be filled with plenty, and your vats will overflow with new wine.
Prov. 10:22 – The blessing of the LORD makes one rich, and He adds no sorrow with it.
Deut. 8:7-13,18 – For the LORD your God is bringing you into a good land, a land of brooks of water, of fountains and springs, that flow out of valleys and hills; a land of wheat and barley, of vines and fig trees and pomegranates, a land of olive oil and honey; a

land in which you will eat bread without scarcity, in which you will lack nothing; a land whose stones are iron and out of whose hills you can dig copper. When you have eaten and are full, then you shall bless the LORD your God for the good land which He has given you. "Beware that you do not forget the LORD your God by not keeping His commandments, His judgments, and His statutes which I command you today, lest when you have eaten and are full, and have built beautiful houses and dwell in them; and when your herds and your flocks multiply, and your silver and your gold are multiplied, and all that you have is multiplied. . . . And you shall remember the LORD your God, for it is He who gives you power to get wealth, that He may establish His covenant which He swore to your fathers, as it is this day."

Ps. 35:27 – Let them shout for joy and be glad, who favor my righteous cause; and let them say continually, "Let the LORD be magnified, who has pleasure in the prosperity of His servant."

2 Cor. 9:8 – And God is able to make all grace abound toward you, that you, always having all sufficiency in all things, may have an abundance for every good work.

Ecc. 10:19 – A feast is made for laughter, and wine makes merry; But money answers everything

1 Tim. 5:8 – But if anyone who does not provide for his own, and especially for those of his household, he has denied the faith and is worse than an unbeliever.

Gleanings From the Word

From many pulpits each Sunday, the faithful are encouraged to give to the work of the Lord. This request is often coupled with a statement communicating that those who give will be blessed. Unfortunately, many givers are never told how they will be blessed, or that it is God's delight to bless them with abundant provisions of finances and valued goods and services.

The Bible presents us with a caring God who challenges us to give with the expectation of reaping a harvest from Him. We are encouraged to sow generously in the anticipation that we will reap bountifully. He is the Lord, our Provider, who is not the least bit scandalized by our desires to live comfortably. He has purposely anointed us with the ability to get wealth and has promised to bless us in a manner so rich that it has no companions of sorrow. The Scriptures even imply that He expects His people to build beautiful homes.

The aforementioned may sound revolutionary to those who have been taught that money is the root of all evil. This is untrue. The *love* of money that is the root of all evil. Money is a neutral commodity that is God's appointed answer for most everything. Any conscientious person knows that money cannot buy health, harmonious relationships, or inner peace. But it does pay for medication to enable us to get well. It helps keep domestic relationships harmonious, because when income is reasonable, there is no reason to argue about family finances. Those who do not have sufficient funds often have less inner peace than those who do, simply because they worry about meeting their obligations. Frankly, the Scriptures imply that healthy family heads who do not provide for their families have denied the power of the faith.

The following references are followed by a brief commentary on what type of harvest can be expected in specific situations:
Prov. 3:9-10 – We tithe with the expectations that God will cause our businesses to overflow with prosperity.
Mk. 10:29-30 – If we relinquish family, friends and property for the sake of our faith in Christ, we can expect a one-hundredfold return in this life. A one-hundredfold return is the equivalent of 10,000 percent interest.
Prov. 19:17 – If we give to the poor, God accepts it as a loan to Him. He is faithful to repay His debt with interest.
Ecc. 11:1-2 – Anything that we give to assist those who are in the

waters of financial adversity will come back to us should we undergo the same. The more violent our storm is, the quicker it will come back from multiple sources.

God graciously invites us all to give with the expectation that He will reward us. His reward is not limited to the level of our need: It is in accordance with His riches in glory. Our provision from heaven will be abundant in quantity and superior in quality to that which we have sown.

Faith's Response

Father God, I am grateful for Your magnanimous nature. As I sow into Your kingdom, I ask that You remind me to anticipate a harvest. When the harvest comes, help me to be sensitive to understand that it came from Your hand, so I can give You the praise.

Chapter Twenty-eight

THE FINAL MARCH

A Golf Story

Like many avid golfers, I thoroughly enjoy watching televised professional tournaments. One of my greatest thrills is to witness the victory march as the victor, with the win assured, makes his way triumphantly from the 18th green. This is a special treat when the winner happens to be a seasoned champion who at last has found relief from a long slump, or someone who has just won his first major tournament. It is gratifying to see them smile as they alternately wave and wipe away tears in response to the cheering crowds.

When Davis Love III won his first major tournament, I found myself with very wet eyes. I was vicariously empathizing with what I imagined his inner emotions to be like. As I watched him receive his trophy and hold it up in victory, my mind went back several years. I again felt the exhilarating joy I had experienced the first time I broke 80 after being rendered legally blind in the aforementioned auto accident. I will never forget how joyous I felt as my foursome congratulated me and smiled as they handed over their cash.

The Word

Heb. 12:22-24 – But you have come to Mount Zion and to the city of the living God, the heavenly Jerusalem, to an innumerable company of angels, to the general assembly and church of the firstborn who are registered in heaven, to God the Judge of all, to the spirits of just men made perfect, to Jesus the Mediator of the new covenant, and to the blood of sprinkling that speaks better things than that of Abel.

2 Tim. 1:8-9 – Therefore do not be ashamed of the testimony of our Lord, nor of me His prisoner, but share with me in the sufferings for the gospel according to the power of God, who has saved us and called us with a holy calling, not according to our works, but according to His own purpose and grace which was given to us in Christ Jesus before time began.

2 Tim. 4:7-8 – I have fought the good fight, I have finished the race, I have kept the faith. Finally, there is laid up for me the crown of righteousness, which the Lord, the righteous Judge, will give to me on that Day, and not to me only but also to all who have loved His appearing.

Gleanings From the Word

Years before I knew Jesus as Savior, I would experience a most unusual occurrence every time I heard music with a military parade cadence. It would hit during a high school football game or while watching the "Rose Bowl Parade" on television. As the music came to my ears, my eyes would fill with tears. At times, the tears would begin to course down my cheeks, and I would mysteriously lose the ability to speak. I secretly fought the urge to break forth into uncontrollable sobs of joy. For decades, I wondered what in the world was wrong with me. What was it about my psyche that would cause me to respond to the sound of fife and drum in such an unorthodox manner? The answer came several years ago, as I was doing a word study on the various words used in the New Testament for the Church.

When I came to Hebrews 12:22-23, I was arrested by the meaning of the Greek word for "general assembly." As I delved through my resource books, the revelation came. The word for "general assembly" is *paneguris*. It has no equivalent in the English language. It is best defined as a victorious army dressed in festal array, parading in review before its supreme commander and chief. As this definition registered upon my spirit, I was riveted with a panoramic vision. I saw all the Lord's redeemed—of all ages, including myself and familiar brothers—marching in glory before the review throne of our supreme commander and chief, the Lord Jesus Christ. Every head was turned toward Him in radiant adoration for the victory that He had granted over all of our foes. I clearly saw that, in spite of all of her sins, blunders and moral improprieties, the Church has been foreordained for greatness from eternity.

This time, I made no effort to contain my tears, nor my sobs of joy. God had granted me a revelation of what had mystified me for years. Before I was born of the Spirit, the Holy Spirit had been deftly working in my heart. He had placed within my psyche a subtle token of the reality that I had been called to march in victory before the Lord at the end of this age. In the eternal realm of the Spirit, before time as we know it began, He had blessed me with a holy calling. It was designed to equip me to serve Him successfully and faithfully, so I could qualify to join the redeemed in our final march before His reviewing platform in heaven.

Experiences and foreordained callings like that which I described above are not atypical in Christians' lives. Most every believer can cite encounters that indicated the wooing presence of the Holy Spirit in their lives prior to their conversions. None of us have been exempted from a responsible calling with which we are to serve our Lord. To this, our wisest response must be to endeavor to fulfill our spiritual vocations faithfully, so we can march proudly on the final day.

The time and effort that it takes to discern one's spiritual calling has eternal rewards. Here are some steps that you might find helpful:

1) Learn what spiritual gifts and callings are possible by studying the Bible and resource materials on that subject.

2) Examine your own desires concerning those gifts and identify what it is that you truly desire to do. God inspires our desires, and very often inklings of our giftings are embedded in our desires.

3) The old saying, "The acorn does not fall far from the tree," is appropriate when attempting to ascertain one's calling. Look under your tree of life: What type of fruit or activity do you find easily falls within the realm of your daily life? It may be hospitality, encouraging the faith of others, or serving the practical needs of your church. It could be that, as you pray for those afflicted with sickness, they frequently become well. Whatever you discover is a regular product of your life is most likely what God has gifted you to do. Give yourself fully to it. Make it a priority in your considerations of what activities you will apply yourself to. Everything that you do each day should be that which will better equip you to fulfill your spiritual destiny.

Faith's Response

Lord, I am so very grateful for the way You drew me to Yourself before I officially welcomed You into my life. Please give me the faith and insight that I need today to best please You and to be a blessing to others. Lord, because of Your help, I know I can joyfully anticipate the day when I will appear before Your throne with the redeemed of all ages.

Chapter Twenty-nine

AMBITION IS LEGAL

A Golf Story

While legally blind from that car accident, I played in the City Championship tournament. I had a strong desire to win, so I prayed and fasted the day prior to the third-round match. It turned out that I had to give my opponent one stroke on each of the three most difficult holes. This perplexed me, because I knew Norm to be a good player. I grumbled to myself, "Sure, I'm blind and they want me to give him three strokes!"

Through the first 12, he was leading by two holes. On the 13th green, he forgot that it was a stroke hole for him and inadvertently picked up when I made par, as he had already made four strokes. Then the other twosome reminded him that it was a stroke hole for him. He sheepishly asked if I would allow him to replace his ball and putt. I sent up a quick prayer to discern if I trusted God enough to place the match in such jeopardy. I smiled a weak "yes," while crying on the inside. He made the putt, so we tied the hole. He maintained his two-hole lead with five left to play. I won two more between 14 and 16, which meant we were tied. Then he won 17, which put me behind by one. At the final tee, his friends encouraged him that he had the win "in the bag." Inwardly, I responded, lovingly of course, "You creeps! We will see about that. I didn't hear the 'fat lady' sing." The flow of my competitive juices intensified, and so did my mental prayer. I beat him on 18, which put us in a playoff. I won the playoff and advanced triumphantly to the semi-finals without a single twitch of guilt for my ambition to be a winner.

The Word

1 Sam. 17:24-33 – And all the men of Israel, when they saw the man (Goliath), fled from him and were dreadfully afraid. So the men of Israel said (to David), "Have you seen this man who has come up? Surely he has come up to defy Israel; and it shall be that the man who kills him the king will enrich with great riches, will give him his daughter, and give his father's house exemption from taxes in Israel." Then David spoke to the men who stood by him, saying, "What shall be done for the man who kills this Philistine and takes away the reproach from Israel? For who is this uncircumcised Philistine, that he should defy the armies of the living God?" And the people answered him in this manner, saying, "So shall it be done for the man who kills him." Now Eliab his oldest brother heard when he spoke to the men; and Eliab's anger was aroused against David, and he said, "Why did you come down here? And with whom have you left those few sheep in the wilderness? I know your pride and the insolence of your heart, for you have come down to see the battle." And David said, "What have I done now? Is there not a cause?" Then he turned from him toward another and said the same thing; and these people answered him as the first ones did. Now when the words which David spoke were heard, they reported them to Saul; and he sent for him. Then David said to Saul, "Let no man's heart fail because of him; your servant will go and fight with this Philistine." And Saul said to David, "You are not able to go against this Philistine to fight with him; for you are a youth, and he a man of war from his youth."
Mk. 10:28-30 – Then Peter began to say to Him, "See, we have left all and followed You." So Jesus answered and said, "Assuredly,

I say to you, there is no one who has left house or brothers or sisters or father or mother or wife or children or lands, for My sake and the gospel's, who shall not receive a hundredfold now in this time—houses and brothers and sisters and mothers and children and lands, with persecutions—and in the age to come, eternal life.

Gleanings From the Word

The ambition to be a winner resides in the breast of every man. Every person who draws breath has an inner drive to advance either in income or title. We all enjoy recognition from our peers when we have achieved something of note. The Lordship of Jesus over our lives does not nullify this drive. To the contrary, it intensifies it. All who embrace the cross of Christ are equipped to become high achievers. We have the Word to instruct us, the Holy Spirit to guide us, and the testimony of the champions of God to inspire us.

King David and the Apostle Peter were both men who were deeply committed to the purposes of God. Though both were willing to sacrifice all for God, they were still compelled by their desires for rewards. They understood that it was legal for spiritually-minded people to have the ambition to advance in life in order to bless their families financially. The Lord did not upbraid them for their ambition. He subtly used it as a motivating factor in getting His purposes accomplished.

David's initial motivation for killing the giant was not religious, nor was it out of ethnic pride. His cause was to win the king's bounty. He had overheard the soldiers talking, as they commented that anyone who killed Goliath would be rewarded with marriage to the king's daughter (hopefully, the pretty one), great riches and tax exemption for his entire family. David asked the men to repeat themselves three different times—he wanted to make sure that he had heard correctly. Once he had a grasp of the reality of the reward, he would not be denied. He pushed through his brother's criticism and King Saul's apprehensions. He boldly announced, "Sir, your problems are over: I'll put this guy down."

Peter reminded Jesus that he and the other apostles had given up everything for Him, and then he unashamedly inquired, "What's in it for us?" The Lord did not rebuke him for the sins of ruthless self-ambition or the love of money. The Master did not patronize Peter with some religious cliché about rewards in the by and by. He knew how to get the best out of His employees: He assured him that all who sacrificed on behalf of the kingdom would receive a one-hundredfold (10,000%) reward in this life, plus eternal life in the future.

It must be noted that the Lord added that persecution would come with the rewards. The persecution arises on two fronts. The first is Satan, who will make every effort to keep Christians swimming in the sea of obscurity. The second source is from uninformed believers who equate piety with poverty and humility with aimless mediocrity.

Do not let either thwart you. The Lord is there to lead you in victory in the marathon of life. When you claim, "I can do all things through Christ who strengthens me," He does not mind giving you tangible fruit to prove what you have accomplished. Go for it!

Faith's Response

Lord, forgive me for ignorantly settling for less than your best. I want to provide for my family in a gracious manner and bring honor to Your name through the notoriety of my achievements. Give me the victory today, and I will lay the trophy at Your feet this evening.

Chapter Thirty
THE THREE BEST
A Golf Story

The three best amateur golfers that I have ever seen are Bill Helman, James "Killer" Walker and Douglas Busby. I treasure each opportunity that I have to play with these men. I have included a brief rundown on each of them.

Bill Helman is an astute businessman in his late 50s who resides in Delray Beach, Florida. His scratch handicap has afforded him the privilege of being paired with some of the greatest names in golf. His prowess in approach shots is phenomenal. I think it is his keen sense of distance, coupled with excellent hands, that makes him so formidable. I enjoy watching his under 50-yard flop shot. He opens his stance with his feet rather close together. His hands are held close into his body. He then takes a three-fourths, U-shaped swing. His hands end at the same height at which they started. His emphasis is on making a firm, smooth snap at the bottom of his down swing. More often than not, the ball will drop dead in legitimate gimme territory.

James Walker is a stately African-American who is near 80 years of age. His home course is Revolution Municipal Golf Course in Charlotte, North Carolina. Both James and my father have been playing there for over 60 years. Mr. Walker is fondly called "Killer" by the players whose pocketbooks have been slaughtered by his ability to use his putter as a Texas wedge. It is absolutely intriguing to watch him withdraw his putter from the bag for 75-yard approaches. The length of the grass and other obstructions never phase him in the least. I really cannot describe how he does it. But he can lag an approach putt closer to the hole than most professionals can with a lofted wedge.

Another great quality Mr. Walker has is his graciousness toward golfers that are having a bad day. I can still hear him as he once remarked to me on such an occasion, "That's okay, Baby. I knows you is a good golfer, and so does the good Lord."

Douglas Busby is a postal clerk who lives in Bessemer, Alabama. I met him there at the Bent Brook Country Club. My father and I were paired up with him and his partner. It was their second round of the day, and I discerned that they had not let the beer cooler in their cart get too lonesome. Douglas is tall and lean and was wearing one of those "Indiana Jones" type of hats. He reminded me a little of an unmade bed. As we introduced ourselves, I sized them up. Frankly, I smelled the brew and thought to myself that I would be locating their lost balls for the rest of the afternoon. By the third hole, I was praising God that I had kept my money in my pocket. Without question, he is the best golfer with whom I have ever played. I have been on the course with him enough to see that his 68 score that first day was no fluke. He has made quite an impression on me. I now wear a hat like his, and were it not for my convictions, I might be tempted to be outfitted with a cooler as well.

The Word

Deut. 6:4 – "Hear, O Israel: The LORD our God, the LORD is one!"

Mk. 12:32 – So the scribe said to Him, "Well said, Teacher. You have spoken the truth, for there is one God, and there is no other but He."

Gen. 1:26 – Then God said, "Let Us make man in Our image, according to Our likeness; let them have dominion over the fish of the sea, over the birds of the air, and over the cattle, over all the earth and over every creeping thing that creeps on the earth."

Ps. 110:1 – The LORD said to my Lord, "Sit at My right hand, Till I make Your enemies Your footstool."

Dan. 7:13-14 – "I was watching in the night visions, and behold, One like the Son of Man, coming with the clouds of heaven! He came to the Ancient of Days, and they brought Him near before Him. Then to Him was given dominion and glory and a kingdom, that all peoples, nations, and languages should serve Him. His dominion is an everlasting dominion, which shall not pass away, and His kingdom the one which shall not be destroyed."

Mt. 3:16-17 – When He had been baptized, Jesus came up immediately from the water; and behold, the heavens were opened to Him, and He saw the Spirit of God descending like a dove and alighting upon Him. And suddenly a voice came from heaven, saying, "This is My beloved Son, in whom I am well pleased."

1 Cor. 6:17 – But he who is joined to the Lord is one spirit with Him.

Eph. 2:18 – For through Him we both have access by one Spirit to the Father.

Gleanings From the Word

The three best acquaintances that everyone can make are God the Father, God the Eternal Son, and God the Holy Spirit. They are called the Trinity because they are one in their unity. As three uniquely distinct Persons, they flow in perfectly harmonious agreement. Though most Christians believe in the Trinity, they find the concept perplexing. The mystery centers around the Scriptures which say that there is one God, and that God is One.

It is confusing because it is our tendency to think numerically when we hear the word *one*. In the Scriptures, "one" is often used to describe unity between separate individuals. Husband and wife are called one, yet they are distinctively different individuals in their sex and function. One passage relates that those who are joined to Jesus in the faith are one spirit with Him. Then, in 1 Corinthians 7:1, it says that we are to cleanse ourselves of all filthiness of spirit. If the aforementioned oneness in spirit indicated a numerical value, it would imply the unthinkable. It is impossible for Jesus to have filthiness in His Spirit. We can only conclude that the phrase "one spirit with Him" refers to unity rather than number.

There are many incidents in the Bible where members of the Godhead are portrayed as functioning simultaneously in the same location. In Daniel, the divine Son of Man was seen receiving an everlasting kingdom from God the Father, the Ancient of Days. When the prophet John baptized Christ, he heard the Father speaking from heaven, and he saw the Holy Spirit coming upon Jesus like a dove. If God the Father, God the Son, and God the Holy Spirit were actually a singular divine person, it would indicate that Jesus was performing simultaneously as a ventriloquist and an illusionist.

During the fourth century A.D., theologians met in council to unravel the confusion. Heretics were denying the separate identities of the three persons of the Godhead, the deity of Jesus and the personhood of the Holy Spirit. The council released the Nicene Creed as the confession of clarification. It relates these truths about the Godhead: "We believe in one God. And in one Lord Jesus Christ, the Son of God, begotten of the Father, light of light, very God of very God, begotten and not made, being of one substance with the Father. And we believe in the Holy Ghost, the Lord and giver of life, who proceedeth from the Father, who with the Father and the Son, is worshipped and glorified, who spake by the prophets."

In my estimation, if our relationship with God does not feature intimate fellowship with each member of the Godhead, it is incomplete.

Faith's Response

Dear Father, I ask You to send the Holy Spirit to lead me into intimate fellowship with each member of the Trinity.

Chapter Thirty-one

MULTIPLE PERSONALITY DISORDER

A Golf Tip

Many weekend golfers suffer from golf's form of a psychological dysfunction called M.P.D. (multiple personality disorder). Its manifestation is their inconsistency in making consecutively good shots. When this occurs, they make statements that could lead one to think they had M.P.D. After a horrendously bad shot followed by an excellent one, they exclaim, "Same guy!" I have one friend who uses the phrase "Good guy/ Nazi." One day, I heard him yell it at least ten times during our round at Heron Bay, where the Honda Classic is held.

There is a cure for this malady which does not require medication or a trip to the psychiatrist's couch. The prescription is to establish a routine for each variety of shot you could make in a round. Then go through the same routine each time you have a particular type of shot. It is wise to base each routine upon what has worked for you in the past. Commit yourself to never make your grip as you are walking to its lie. When you hurriedly walk up to a ball and smack it, you might likely hear another smack as it hits a tree or the water. Here are two sample routines: For an uphill lie, choose a club that will get the ball up high enough to negotiate the hill with optimum distance toward your target. Set your stance so your shoulders seem parallel with the slope. Bend you knees to the extent necessary to enable you to swing through without needing to jerk up. Set your grip and take a practice swing. Step up to the ball, taking the same stance and shoulder position. Keep your left eye behind the ball and swing. When putting, examine your lie from four viewpoints. Determine the best path and set your stance. Make practice swings until you sense that you have the feel for the correct speed and distance. Never make a practice swing if you are not set up exactly as you will be for your actual putt. Why? Because your brain sends messages to your body for muscle memory when you are thinking about a particular shot. If you are not set up correctly, the wrong messages are sent to your body. Now set up for the putt and hole it.

End your M.P.D. by consistently keeping the same set up routine.

The Word

1 Pet. 5:8 – Be sober, be vigilant; because your adversary the devil walks about like a roaring lion, seeking whom he may devour.
Eph. 6:11-17 – Put on the whole armor of God, that you may be able to stand against the wiles of the devil. For we do not wrestle against flesh and blood, but against principalities, against powers, against the rulers of the darkness of this age, against spiritual hosts of wickedness in the heavenly places. Therefore take up the whole armor of God, that you may be able to withstand in the evil day, and having done all, to stand. Stand therefore, having girded your waist with truth, having put on the breastplate of righteousness, and having shod your feet with the preparation of the gospel of peace; above all, taking the shield of faith with which you will be able to quench all the fiery darts of the wicked one. And take the helmet of salvation, and the sword of the Spirit, which is the word of God.

Rev. 12:10-11 – Then I heard a loud voice saying in heaven, "Now salvation, and strength, and the kingdom of our God, and the power of His Christ have come, for the accuser of our brethren, who accused them before our God day and night, has been cast down. And they overcame him by the blood of the Lamb and by the word of their testimony, and they did not love their lives to the death."

Gleanings From the Word

Our third daughter Holly was sickly until age four. Routine childhood sicknesses that other children would breeze through became long-term arduous ordeals for her. My wife was praying about it, and the Lord spoke these words to her heart: "Remember she almost died at birth. She is now afflicted with the spirit of infirmity and death." When my wife told me about her revelation, it rang in my spirit as an authentic message from God. Several weeks later, our daughter became ill. She was fully awake as I took her into my arms and prayed, "In the name of Jesus, I command this spirit of infirmity and death to leave now." When I did this, Holly jerked as if convulsing and then passed out. This startled us, but we had inner confidence that God was in control. Therefore, we began to sing hymns that extolled the attributes of the blood of Jesus. After about 10 minutes, she came to and smiled up at us cheerfully. She did not have another serious episode of illness for the balance of her childhood. Today, she is an energetic wife and career woman who is blessed with excellent health.

In this life, all of us are intermittently faced with challenges in our relationships, our personalities, our finances and our health. For the most part, these things are resolved as we cover our lives with the Christian disciplines of prayer, praise, Bible study and meaningful fellowship with other believers. However, there are times when solutions elude us, and troubles become mystifying in their intensity and duration. When this occurs, it is not a signal that

God has abandoned us to a life of perplexing misery. At times, the answer is found when we approach the matter through biblical principles of spiritual warfare.

When a particular trial of life becomes cruelly exaggerated, there is a reasonable possibility that it is energized by satanic spiritual forces. One of the gifts of the Holy Spirit is called discerning of spirits. This gift implies that there are spiritual powers that can covertly influence our lives until they are discerned and dealt with. Satan is portrayed in Scripture as a lion who roams about seeking ways to disrupt and devour our enjoyment of life. We may not see him or his demonic cohorts with the naked eye, but we can discern when they are at work.

It would be erroneous to interpret all problematic situations as energized by demons, but any circumstance can be. Afflictions in our health, relationships, finances and emotions which are not eased by time and prayer could be of demonic origin. When this occurs, label it with a personal name derived from the nature of its activity. For instance, if it is unreasonable depression, call it "spirit of depression." If it is the inability to pay your bills when your income would be adequate for others, call it "demon of poverty." Once the identification is made, firmly address it like you would a stray dog that was soiling your lawn. Enhance your rebuke with phrases that enforce what the Word of God says in relation to what the blood of Jesus has done for you as a child of God. Then end your prayer with a time of praise and thanksgiving for the victory.

I have another example from my own experience. I loved the Lord and my family, but the tranquillity of our home was often disrupted through my explosions of impatient irritability. I thought it was just a weakness of my personality, and for years it remained the subject of prayers of repentance. After one bizarre episode, I attacked it as a wicked spiritual entity. There was an instant change. Our home is now a haven of peace, with only minor displays of my temper. Today's Faith's Response offers the prayer that I used. If you discern that you are in need, interject the name of your particular problem.

Faith's Response

You demon of impatient anger, you will not disrupt my life for one more moment. I command you to leave my home and person now, in the name of Jesus. Through the blood of Christ, I have been set apart and made holy to God. Satan has no place in me, nor power over me. All of his claims on my personality have been voided by the blood of the Lamb. This confession of the blood of Jesus has set me free from every influence from Satan's kingdom. I thank God that I have been set free.

Chapter Thirty-two

THE GAMES PEOPLE PLAY

A Golf Tip

One of the intriguing aspects of golf is that it is a sport which can be enhanced by diverse game formats. Playing with an accompanying game helps with one's concentration and heightens the enjoyment of a round. A few common game formats are described below:

Fox and Hounds is played in match or hole by hole play. The player or team who carries the lead through or gains the lead at the ninth or 18th hole wins that particular nine. When a player or team win a hole, they become the fox, and those attempting to overtake them are the hounds in pursuit. In the case of a tie, whoever was the fox for the most holes in that nine wins. If this too is a tie, the lowest score, less handicap strokes, for that particular nine holes wins. In another variation of the game, the fox can opt to choose his partner for the next chase. This is normally done after he has seen their tee shots.

In **Greenies and Sandies,** points or a monetary unit are won each time a player makes a green in regulation, or makes par even though he had a sand shot. Other "ies" can be included. **Barkies and Wateries** occur when par is made after a ball hits a tree or the water. **Offies and Arnies** occur when the ball was holed from off the green, or when par was made though the fairway was missed and the green was not made in regulation.

In **Play it Again, Sam,** a better player must replay a given number of shots at the request of their opponent. The number of request for replays that can be requested by the lesser player is determined by the numerical difference in their handicaps. A player who carries a handicap of 18 could request eight replays from an opponent with a handicap of ten during the round. The strategic time for each request is after a good shot has been made from a troublesome lie.

A **Nassau** is a three-part bet in which a player can win or lose a pre-set amount of money on the front nine, the back nine, and the overall round. A five-dollar Nassau would mean that five dollars was wagered on each of the three respective parts. A player could win or lose no more than 15 dollars.

In **Scramble,** each member of a team hits shots from his team's best previous lie from the tee and on through the ball being holed. The low total score wins the round.

In **Short Putts**, a player is penalized a predetermined amount of points or money each time he leaves a putt for par or better short.

The Word

Gal. 5:19-20 – Now the works of the flesh are evident, which are: adultery, fornication, uncleanness, lewdness, idolatry, sorcery, hatred, contentions, jealousies, outbursts of wrath, selfish ambitions, dissensions, heresies. . . .

1 Sam. 15:23 – "For rebellion is as the sin of witchcraft, And stubbornness is as iniquity and idolatry. Because you have rejected the word of the LORD, He also has rejected you from being king."

Col. 3:19-21 – Husbands, love your wives and do not be bitter toward them. Children, obey your parents in all things, for this is well pleasing to the Lord. Fathers, do not provoke your children, lest they become discouraged.

Jdg. 16:16 – And it came to pass, when she pestered him daily with her words and pressed him, so that his soul was vexed to death.

James 3:13-18 – Who is wise and understanding among you? Let him show by good conduct that his works are done in the meekness of wisdom. But if you have bitter envy and self-seeking in your hearts, do not boast and lie against the truth. This wisdom does not descend from above, but is earthly, sensual, demonic. For where envy and self-seeking exist, confusion and every evil thing are there. But the wisdom that is from above is first pure, then peaceable, gentle, willing to yield, full of mercy and good fruits, without partiality and without hypocrisy. Now the fruit of righteousness is sown in peace by those who make peace.

Gleanings From the Word

There is a game which we all play that can become destructive if played too frequently. It is called *manipulation.* In its extreme form, it wrecks relationships and is a primary factor in wounding children to the point that they are dysfunctional as adults. It is benign when entered cheerfully and all concerned know that the game is in play. It is dangerous when used as a perpetual tool to impose one's plans and viewpoints on others.

Manipulation is the effort which is used through the force of one's personality to get others to comply with their clear or hidden agendas. The word *manipulation* is not a biblical term. There is, however, another word that describes a sinful work of the flesh which is surprisingly akin to it. The term is *sorcery* or *witchcraft.* Witchcraft can be described as the effort to get others to behave in a certain manner through the use of covert mental or spiritual powers. It is sinful in that its primary goal is to establish control over other's actions without consideration of the will of God or the other party's wishes. In 1 Samuel 15:23, two common motivations for manipulation are defined as witchcraft and idolatry. They are rebellion and stubbornness. A rebellious person seeks to establish his or her will in a situation where the authority belongs to another. A stubborn individual values his or her own opinions higher than the thoughts of others.

Both men and women play the manipulation game, but their tactics tend to vary somewhat. Men are at times vague in their initial communication about what they expect. If they do not obtain compliance that meets their expectations, they often react either through an intimidating outburst of verbal abuse or sullen pouting. For instance, a child who does not perform an assigned task in a manner that pleases his father could spark the father to scream repeatedly, citing the child's stupid ineptness. Or, he could slip into a state of seething anger in which he sullenly glares disapprovingly at the offender for days on end. Children raised without routine, strong paternal affirmation can become misshapen in their sense of self-worth.

Women are masterful in their ability to manipulate through their verbal skills and body language. A husband offers a suggestion for an activity that is unattractive to his wife. She responds with a roll of her eyes, which communicates that his thought is ludicrous. If the objectionable plan is pursued, she might feign a headache or shed purposed tears. Or, if a family member does not comply with her agenda, she might respond with statements that question their love for her or her own worth as a member of the family: "If you really loved me, you would. . . ." "I guess I am the worst wife in the world. You would have been better off to marry someone else." The family responds by complying with her desires in order to reinforce their love for her and her value to them. When children are raised in an environment in which their emotions are kept on edge by their love for a parent being questioned, they can mature into dysfunctional insecurity.

No one has the right to assert dominion over the destinies of others through the continual mind games of manipulation.

Faith's Response

Lord, I have been guilty of the sin of using illegitimate methods to manipulate people and situations. I acknowledge that You often indicate Your will through the plans and ideas of others. I repent of my sin against You and those I have coerced though my unfair tactics. From this point on, I will attempt to be sensitive to Your will as it is expressed by the alternative wishes of those around me.

Chapter Thirty-three

SUPERSTITIONS

A Golf Tip

I have noticed that the performance of some golf enthusiasts is subject to a variety of superstitions. Some panic if they lose their "lucky ball." Others begin to twitch if they run out of balls of a favored brand or number. Some prognosticate the type of round they will have by the quality of their starting holes. If they score badly on the first several holes, they take it as an omen of the inevitability of a high final score. I know of one player who occasionally loses cart partners due to his refusal to wash his one charmed golf outfit.

Success in a round of golf is as dependent upon our mental attitudes as it is our playing skill. If you have intertwined your hope of success with any superstitious attachments, you would be best served to renounce them. The game is complex enough on its own. No one needs to labor under the weight of myths relating to the source of their previous successes.

The Word

Deut. 18:10-14 – There shall not be found among you anyone who makes his son or his daughter pass through the fire, or one who practices witchcraft, or a soothsayer, or one who interprets omens, or a sorcerer, or one who conjures spells, or a medium, or a spiritist, or one who calls up the dead. For all who do these things are

139

an abomination to the LORD, and because of these abominations
the LORD your God drives them out from before you. You shall be
blameless before the LORD your God. For these nations which
you will dispossess listened to soothsayers and diviners; but as for
you, the LORD your God has not appointed such for you.

Isa. 47:12-15 – Stand now with your enchantments and the multitude of your sorceries, in which you have labored from your youth.
Perhaps you will be able to profit, perhaps you will prevail. You are
wearied in the multitude of your counsels; let now the astrologers,
the stargazers, and the monthly prognosticators Stand up and save
you from what shall come upon you. Behold, they shall be as
stubble, the fire shall burn them; they shall not deliver themselves
from the power of the flame; it shall not be a coal to be warmed by,
nor a fire to sit before! Thus shall they be to you with whom you
have labored, your merchants from your youth; they shall wander
each one to his quarter. No one shall save you.

Acts 16:16-19 – Now it happened, as we went to prayer, that a certain slave girl possessed with a spirit of divination met us, who
brought her masters much profit by fortune-telling. This girl followed Paul and us, and cried out, saying, "These men are the servants of the Most High God, who proclaim to us the way of
salvation." And this she did for many days. But Paul, greatly an-
noyed, turned and said to the spirit, "I command you in the name
of Jesus Christ to come out of her." And he came out that very
hour. But when her masters saw that their hope of profit was gone,
they seized Paul and Silas and dragged them into the marketplace
to the authorities.

Acts 19:18-20 – And many who had believed came confessing and
telling their deeds. Also, many of those who had practiced magic
brought their books together and burned them in the sight of all.
And they counted up the value of them, and it totaled fifty thousand pieces of silver. So the word of the Lord grew mightily and
prevailed.

Superstitions

2 Cor. 5:17 – Therefore, if anyone is in Christ, he is a new creation; old things have passed away; behold, all things have become new.

Gleanings From the Word

Superstitions have no part in the lives of those who esteem the name of Jesus. The Word of God contains scores of references which reveal that it is forbidden for believers to perceive that their destinies can be predicted or influenced by any agency beyond the providential will of God. Casual adherence to superstitions can hinder a person's progress in productive faith in God and His Word.

This truth is borne out in the case of the Christians of ancient Ephesus. After they confessed their involvement with occult mysticism and burned their libraries of related books, the Word of God began to empower their lives in a new dimension. Reliable scholars state that a portion of the books they destroyed were called "Ephesian scrolls." These were the equivalent of the daily horoscopes that can be found in modern newspapers. Even if astrology had factual information, it would not be applicable to Christians. We are not sentenced to live under the dominion of the alleged astrological influences of our birthdays. We were deemed new creations in Christ on the day of our respective conversions. As new creations, we are designed to flow in the character of Christ—not the starry host.

A visit to a fortuneteller and a reading that is laced with elements of truth does not indicate that the source of the revelation is spiritually legitimate. The fortunetelling girl who followed Paul's company as they went to their daily prayers was accurate in her statements about their mission. They were sent by God to show the inhabitants of Philippi the way to salvation. However, inspiration for this proclamation did not originate with God: It was the activity

141

of an evil spirit of divination. When it was expelled from the girl, she lost her ability to tell fortunes.

Deuteronomy 18 lists a number of forbidden superstitious practices. I have grouped them by similarity and have offered definitions for each group:

Witchcraft and soothsayers use divination to determine past or future events.

Sorcerers and those who conjure spells can be defined as anyone who puts spells on the unwitting or those who offer "blessed" amulets and potions to ward off evil and to ensure health and success.

A medium, spiritist or one who calls up the dead is a practitioner who channels demonic spirits to provide hidden information to an inquirer. They allege that the voices which come through them are those of the dead.

One who interprets omens is anyone who attempts to provide prophetic insights through natural events. Astrologers and tea leaf readers would fall into this category.

Christians who have been beguiled into these realms of satanic deception need to repent and renounce their involvement.

Faith's Response

Father, I repent of my interest in the forbidden realm of the occult. I renounce it as sin and ask You to liberate me from its spiritually defiling influences.

Chapter Thirty-four

MULLIGANS AND GIMMES

A Golf Tip

The two most frequently requested favors that golfers ask of their foursomes is for mulligans and gimmes. A *mulligan* is a re-played shot which is taken after a poor tee shot. A *gimme* is a putt which is conceded as holed because it appears too close to the hole to miss. At times, players ask for them. Though I took my share of them when I first started golfing, I rarely take them now. I have come to the conviction that mulligans and gimmes are very decep-tive, because they give you an inaccurate impression of your real scoring ability. Gimmes rob one of the opportunity to cultivate prowess in short putts. The reality usually sets in when one gives his handicap as a 15 and shoots 22 over par when other players in-sist that there be neither mulligans or gimmes. If you are addicted to them, keep it reasonable. A single mulligan can be allowed on the first tee only. Gimmes should never be given if they are more than a putter head's length from the hole. When one that is simply inside the leather of the shaft is granted, you are conceding one of the most difficult putts in the game.

The Word

Num. 6:23-26 – Speak to Aaron and his sons, saying, "This is the way you shall bless the children of Israel. Say to them: 'The

143

LORD bless you and keep you; The LORD make His face shine upon you, And be gracious to you; The LORD lift up His countenance upon you, And give you peace.'"

Gen. 39:20-23 – Then Joseph's master took him and put him into the prison, a place where the king's prisoners were confined. And he was there in the prison. But the LORD was with Joseph and showed him mercy, and He gave him favor in the sight of the keeper of the prison. And the keeper of the prison committed to Joseph's hand all the prisoners who were in the prison; whatever they did there, it was his doing. The keeper of the prison did not look into anything that was under Joseph's authority, because the LORD was with him; and whatever he did, the LORD made it prosper.

Ps. 5:12 – For You, O LORD, will bless the righteous; with favor You will surround him as with a shield.

Prov. 19:12 – The king's wrath is like the roaring of a lion, But his favor is like dew on the grass.

Prov. 22:1 – A good name is to be chosen rather than great riches, loving favor rather than silver and gold.

Ps. 119:58 – I entreated Your favor with my whole heart; be merciful to me according to Your word.

Ps. 106:4-5 – Remember me, O LORD, with the favor You have toward Your people; Oh, visit me with Your salvation, that I may see the benefit of Your chosen ones, that I may rejoice in the gladness of Your nation, that I may glory with Your inheritance.

Ps. 112:5 – A good man deals graciously (shows favor) and lends; he will guide his affairs with discretion.

Gleanings From the Word

There were three single women in my church who had recently leased a home in a nice section of our city. They came to me and asked if I knew where they might get furnishings at a reduced price, as they had exhausted their resources on the security deposit and the first and last month's rent requirement. I instructed them to begin to confess, among themselves, that they had favor with everyone they met. I explained that the Lord's favor could cause complete strangers to deal with them very graciously for no apparent reason. Before they left, I prayed a blessing of favor over them. The next Sunday, they gleefully reported to the whole church what had happened as a result. Their landlord happened to be an antique dealer. When she came over to check on the girls, she noticed that their furnishings were sparse. She inquired about it, and they told her about their temporary shortage of funds. She smiled and told them that her warehouse was overrun with household goods. She then asked if it would be all right if she stored a few things at their home. They gladly consented. By the end of the week, she had furnished the entire house with exquisite antiques ranging from Persian carpets, to brass beds, and the finest of china. Surely, the Lord's favor is better than silver or gold, because its value does not fluctuate, and it is limitless in its capacity to provide.

The Hebrew word for favor means to turn one's face toward someone. The Bible implies that when God favors a person, the glory of His countenance shines down upon him or her. It makes them distinctively attractive to others, and people begin to show them uncharacteristic favor. When God graces you, people will go out of their way to treat you far more graciously than they would others. It can cause you to prosper in the most adverse of circumstances. Joseph was a slave in Egypt. He had been betrayed by his brothers and was a member of the Jewish race, which was held in contempt by the Egyptians. Yet he rose to a position where he was second in power only to the Pharaoh. Why? He had the favor of the Lord. There is not a person living who does not need favor. No matter how gifted or wealthy a person might be, they still enjoy being favored with kind gestures and courtesy.

How do you appropriate the favor of God? It is simple: You ask for it in faith and sow it into the lives of others. As new covenant believers, we can safely assume that it is God's will for us, because, under the old covenant, He commanded that the priest routinely bless all of the Israelites with a prayer for favor. King David intermittently requested it in prayer, and then subsequently thanked the Lord that He had granted him favor. As Christians, we have a better covenant, one that is based upon better promises and officiated by a better High Priest, Jesus. God's promises to us are superior to the ones given to Israel. Ours include all of theirs, plus the ones He gave to us. If you are not trusting God for His favor in your life, you are shortchanging yourself.

Specifically ask the Lord for favor in every area of your life where you need it. As an employee, you need favor from your employer to get raises and better than fair perks. If your relationship with your spouse has been rocky, you would do well to pray that he or she would favor you with newlywed affection. After you have prayed for favor, go forth into your day with the anticipation that you are going to receive it at every juncture. Then follow up by going out of your way to deal graciously with others. If you sow the seeds of favor, you will reap a harvest of the same.

Faith's Response

Lord, You are so good. This is the day that Your favor is going to begin to set me apart as Your child in a new dimension. I believe that people are going to go out of their way to treat me in a gracious manner. As a token of my faith, I am going to seek opportunities to show favor to those around me.

Chapter Thirty-five
THE ALPHA AND OMEGA
A Golf Tip

For years, I had the difficulty of either hitting my shots too thin or too fat. I came up with a self-cure remedy that I call the "alpha and omega." In this technique, I endeavor to make contact with the ball at the exact location on the club where the ball was positioned before my back swing. Though I follow through, it is my aim to bottom out my down swing at the same height which the club face began in my initial setup.

I view my intended target line and then place the club head right on that line. The ball is positioned parallel to the club head's sweetest spot. While doing this, I bend my knees sufficiently enough to prevent the necessity of lifting my body to avoid hitting it fat. At the same time, I position my feet close enough to the ball to ensure that I will not have to reach for it in order to make full contact. I take one more look at my target and then take a compact backswing that tends to feel as though I am making a three-quarters swing. I keep my head down with my left eye behind the ball. My concentration then transfers to striking the ball at the same swing depth and point on the club face which I initially envisioned as my ending target. I try to stay down in my knees and with my head until the finishing follow through draws them upward. This technique has minimized my number of thin and fat shots. It has also served to enable me to become proficient at hitting fairway woods and long irons out of fairway bunkers and waste areas.

147

The Word

Rev. 22:13 – I am the Alpha and the Omega, the Beginning and the End, the First and the Last.

Col. 1:16-18 – For by Him all things were created that are in heaven and that are on earth, visible and invisible, whether thrones or dominions or principalities or powers. All things were created through Him and for Him. And He is before all things, and in Him all things consist. And He is the head of the body, the church, who is the beginning, the firstborn from the dead, that in all things He may have the preeminence.

1 Cor. 15:28 – Now when all things are made subject to Him, then the Son Himself will also be subject to Him who put all things under Him, that God may be all in all.

1 Cor. 3:21 – Therefore let no one boast in men. For all things are yours. . . .

Rom. 8:32 – He who did not spare His own Son, but delivered Him up for us all, how shall He not with Him also freely give us all things?

2 Cor. 9:8 – And God is able to make all grace abound toward you, that you, always having all sufficiency in all things, may have an abundance for every good work.

1 Jn. 2:1 – My little children, these things I write to you, so that you may not sin. And if anyone sins, we have an Advocate with the Father, Jesus Christ the righteous.

Rom. 8:33-34 – Who shall bring a charge against God's elect? It is God who justifies. Who is he who condemns? It is Christ who died, and furthermore is also risen, who is even at the right hand of God, who also makes intercession for us.

Gleanings From the Word

Jesus of Nazareth is the eternal Alpha and Omega. For those

who trust Him, He is the beginning and end, the first and the last. He is our all and all, who is in all. We begin each day's schedule with the motivation of representing His excellent character to the world. We look forward to the sense of His approbation that can certainly come to us at the end of a busy day.

It was He who initiated the existence of all creation. In the beginning, all was made by Him and for Him, with our benefit and enjoyment on His mind. He holds all that we see together through the power of His Word. He will continue to do so until the end, when He proclaims that time is no more and that it is time to begin to make all things new.

Should Satan, the accuser, bring an indictment against us, Jesus, our Advocate, is the first and last to plead our case in the heavenly court. No matter how true the charges against us, we are liberated when He has completed His masterful defense. He has assumed responsibility for our actions and has paid our penalty with His own blood. He is the wisest of all lawyers, so He approves of a jury consisting of our peers who have gone to heaven before us. Jury tampering is the order of the day. Each member is bought with the Blood and reminded that they once stood in our place. The words of our Advocate end all disputes, for His Father is the eternal judge who is prejudiced against the prosecutor and hold him in everlasting contempt of court.

When our loved ones and friends forsake us, He remains our comforter and friend after the last one has gone. If famine or sickness strikes, we need not be alarmed. It may be real, but it is not final. No lack or malady can consume His supply of provision and divine health, which have no end. Finally, as death's dark shroud begins to overtake us, it is the beginning and not the end. We will soon get our first glimpse of the light of His glorious kingdom, which will end the need of day and night eternally.

Faith's Response

Lord Jesus, I praise you for being my beginning and end. You are the Alpha and Omega. I choose to bless Your name with my first and last breaths of each day.

Chapter Thirty-six

YOUR APPOINTED TIME

A Golf Tip

Punctuality is a virtue that golfers need to cultivate. Your appointed tee time is not synonymous with when you are to arrive at the course. Most good courses require that all members of a group check in at least 20 minutes prior to their tee time. It is also important that players be punctual in their pace of play. A foursome should be able to complete a round within four hours. A round is far more enjoyable, and scores are generally lower, when a good pace is maintained. The following guidelines are those which my groups use to ensure a courteous pace of play:

1) Arrive at the course in plenty of time to hit warm up balls and pay for the round. Allow approximately 40 minutes prior to tee time.

2) Decide the order of play and any teams or wagers before arriving at the first tee.

3) Try to avoid taking practice swings while on the tee. Take them off to the side while you are awaiting your turn.

4) Do not hit mulligans.

5) While others in your group are making their shots, be walking to your ball with possible club selections in hand. Set up and hit your ball as soon as it is your turn.

6) On the green, study your line while others are putting. Leave the green briskly, as soon as the hole is finished.

151

7) Always allow faster and smaller groups to play through. On par threes, invite the group behind to hit up.

8) If you have accumulated more than seven strokes before reaching the green, take a two stroke penalty and drop at the 150 yard marker or pick up.

The Word

Hab. 2:3 – For the vision is yet for an appointed time; but at the end it will speak, and it will not lie. Though it tarries, wait for it; because it will surely come, it will not tarry.

Ps. 31:14-15 – But as for me, I trust in You, O LORD; I say, "You are my God." My times are in Your hand; deliver me from the hand of my enemies, and from those who persecute me.

Ps. 102:11-12 – My days are like a shadow that lengthens, and I wither away like grass. But You, O LORD, shall endure forever, and the remembrance of Your name to all generations.

Isa. 40:26 – Lift up your eyes on high, and see who has created these things, who brings out their host by number; He calls them all by name, by the greatness of His might and the strength of His power; not one is missing.

Heb. 9:27 – And as it is appointed for men to die once, but after this the judgment.

2 Cor. 5:10 – For we must all appear before the judgment seat of Christ, that each one may receive the things done in the body, according to what he has done, whether good or bad.

Rev. 20:11-15 – Then I saw a great white throne and Him who sat on it, from whose face the earth and the heaven fled away. And there was found no place for them. And I saw the dead, small and great, standing before God, and books were opened. And another book was opened, which is the Book of Life. And the dead were judged according to their works, by the things which were written in the books. The sea gave up the dead who were in it, and Death and Hades delivered up the dead who were in them. And they were judged, each one according to his works. Then Death and Hades were cast into the lake of fire. This is the second death. And anyone not found written in the Book of Life was cast into the lake of fire.

Ps. 74:20 – Have respect to the covenant; for the dark places of the earth are full of the haunts of cruelty.

2 Cor. 6:2 – For He says: "In an acceptable time I have heard you, And in the day of salvation I have helped you." Behold, now is the accepted time; behold, now is the day of salvation.

Rom. 10:9-10 – If you confess with your mouth the Lord Jesus and believe in your heart that God has raised Him from the dead, you will be saved. For with the heart one believes unto righteousness, and with the mouth confession is made unto salvation.

Gleanings From the Word

God is always punctual in keeping His appointed times for all matters pertaining to His creation. His punctuality is demonstrated each day and night through the starry host. Astronomers can predict the placement of a star scores of years in advance. News broadcasts can tell us the exact time when the sun will rise in the East on any given day. How? Because the heavens are controlled by One who personally orchestrates the path of each star as they move with exact precision.

He also has set three appointments with each one of us. The first, and the longest in duration, is the time He has allotted for His Holy Spirit to draw us into salvation. He has never obligated Himself to strive indefinitely with stubborn indecision. When a person senses that God is speaking to them about eternal matters, wisdom dictates a prompt response. No one has the guarantee that he or she will have another opportunity. Our other two divine appointments are the moment of our death and our scheduled appearance before the judgment throne of God. The habitually tardy will be on time for these two appointments. God has spoken. Our times are in His hands, and He has appointed that each of us will die. After that, we will meet Him at the judgment.

The question is, are you ready? This is not a matter than one should approach casually. Some claim that they are not sure that Jesus is the only way. Therefore, they want to explore other spiritual disciplines so they can make the choice that is right for them. A cursory look at the conditions in non-Christian nations should help one make a quick decision for Christ. The value of Hinduism can be seen as people starve while cattle roam India's streets. Apparently, as some of their ancient holy men meditated, mystical voices spoke and instructed them on holiness. "Do not eat the holy cattle. Kiss the cobras and worship the monkeys, as they too are holy." Animistic practices like voodoo have reduced Haiti and other nations to abject poverty. Islam leads the way in threatening the world with terrorism. The Buddhists and Taoists of the Far East are long on contemplation and short on acts of mercy. Seldom, if ever, does one hear that these religions have organized relief efforts to aid the victims of natural disasters in foreign nations. On the other hand, wherever there is human need, you can likely find those whom Christ has called to minister His mercy. Perhaps today is your appointed time to give the Lord your life.

Faith's Response

Father, I believe that Jesus is the Son of God and that You raised Him from the dead. I repent of my many sins and ask You to forgive me and to cleanse me from them. I now submit my life to You, Lord Jesus, and ask You to come into my heart and to be my Savior and Lord.